2.²⁵

D0378464

10
Fastest-Growing
SOUTHERN BAPTIST
SUNDAY SCHOOLS

10
Fastest-Growing
SOUTHERN BAPTIST
SUNDAY
SCHOOLS

EUGENE SKELTON

Broadman Press / Nashville, Tennessee

© 1974 ● Broadman Press
All rights reserved
4265-15
ISBN:0-8054-6515-4
Library of Congress Catalogue Card Number: 73-83831
Dewey Decimal Classification: 286.06
Printed in the United States of America

To

Ann

who encourages me
and inspires me

Contents

10
Fastest-Growing
SOUTHERN BAPTIST
SUNDAY SCHOOLS

**Sandy Creek Baptist Church is called "the mother church of Southern Baptists."
It's cold outside but warm inside.**

1
Seeing Our Heritage of Reaching People

Sandy Creek Baptist Church
Randolph County, North Carolina

Reaching people for Bible study, for Christ, and for church membership is nothing new for Southern Baptists. They always have been a people dedicated to the belief that men need Christ and marked by an untiring zeal in taking Christ to every possible person. From the beginning of the modern Sunday School movement in America, Southern Baptists have led the way in the development of methods and materials for better Bible teaching. They have also been pacesetters in growing larger Sunday Schools to reach more people.

The commitment to reach people is the characteristic attitude of Southern Baptist people, coming to them as a heritage from their separate Baptist forebears and from the mother church of the separates, the Sandy Creek Baptist Church of Randolph County, North Carolina.

"The neighborhood was alarmed and the Spirit of God listed to blow as a mighty rushing wind." This description of the life and activity of the Sandy Creek Church was written more than two hundred years ago. Those are the words of Morgan Edwards telling of his visit to the church in 1772. Who was Morgan Edwards? What and where was Sandy Creek, the church he spoke of? What has that to do with fast-growing churches and Sunday Schools today?

Morgan Edwards was a native of Wales, but came to America in 1761 to be the pastor of the Baptist church of Philadelphia. There he labored for ten years. In 1770 he resigned his pastorate and devoted his time during the next several years to gathering materials for a history of the Baptists of all America, traveling through the colonies and collecting such information as he could from church books and other documents. This information he carefully and neatly set down in notebooks, one for each colony, most of which have been preserved.

In 1772 he visited North Carolina. He traveled from church to church, writing accounts of each one, including his impressions of them. One church was so unusual that his amazement was unbounded. Of this church he wrote at length — Sandy Creek Separate Baptist Church.

The church was located in what was then a part of Orange County but now is Randolph County, North Carolina. It's pastor was Shubal Stearns, an extremely unique person. In 1741, with sixteen members, he organized the church; it increased in two years to 606 members. Edwards describes it:

The fall after Braddock's defeat (November 22, 1755) the following persons came from Opekon, in Virginia and settled in the neighborhood of *Sandy Creek,* viz.: Rev. Shubal Stearns and wife, Daniel Marshall and wife, Joseph Breed and wife, Shubal Stearnes Senr. and his wife, Ebenezer Stearnes and wife, Enis Stinson and wife, Peter Stearnes and wife, Jonathan Polk and wife: the same year they built a little meeting house near the present, where they administered the Lord's Supper. Soon after the neighbourhood was alarmed and the Spirit of God listed to blow as a mighty rushing wind insomuch that in three years time they had increased to three churches, consisting upwards of 900 communicants, Viz: Sandy Creek, Abot's Creek, Deep River.

The most remarkable events are these: (1) It is a mother church, nay a grandmother, and a great grandmother. All the separatist baptists sprang hince: not only eastward toward the sea, but westward toward the great river Mississippi, but northward to Virginia and southward to South Carolina and Georgia. The word went forth from this sion, and great was the company of them who published it, insomuch that her converts were as the drops of morning dew.

The church and its people went near and far proclaiming the Word of God to those who would listen. The church grew. Soon after its organization, it began to organize branches in every direction. These branches likewise grew and organized still more like themselves. The gospel spread like wildfire through the western North Carolina region and from there north to Virginia and to the south as well, into upper South Carolina and Georgia.

What was the principal characteristic of this church? This question is easy to answer. The church saw reaching people for Jesus Christ as its main business. Called an "enthusiastical sect" by many, the secret of Sandy Creek, Shubal Stearnes, and the churches that sprang from their vision, was a commitment to the idea that Christ had called them to reach people for him. Reaching people for Christ was their reason for existence, way or style of life.

Not far from the Sandy Creek church, still active on the same site (the grave of Shubal Stearnes is in the churchyard), stands a sign erected by the state of North Carolina. "Sandy Creek," it says, "the mother church of Southern Baptists." Well might the sign so read, for Stearnes and the Sandy Creek church bequeathed to Baptists the spirit of reaching people for Christ. That spirit in a church today results in reaching people for Bible study and for Christ. When that spirit prevails, a church has a growing Sunday School.

Should one like Morgan Edwards visit churches today — not in the Carolinas alone, but anywhere in America — he would find many like Sandy Creek. He would find churches committed to reaching people — and reaching them. In widely separated places he could visit churches with stories as remarkable and as unusual as that of Sandy Creek. Some of these churches would be located in the open country, as were nearly all churches then. Many, however, would be located in the great city places or their nearby suburban areas.

A Morgan Edwards of today could not confine his search to one area; he would need to go into every region of the country — North, South, East, and West. In all these parts of the country churches are reaching greater numbers of people. Sunday Schools are growing. More and more people are involved in Bible study programs week by week.

Middle River Baptist Church, Baltimore, Maryland

For his first visit today's Morgan Edwards would not need to travel far from Philadelphia. He could stop at Baltimore where he would find Middle River Baptist Church. Tasting its spirit, he would feel himself at home. It is a "reaching people" church.

When James E. Willey became pastor of this church in March, 1971, the church was reaching about six hundred in its Bible teaching program. It had an enrollment of approximately fifteen hundred. Two years later, in 1973, Sunday School enrollment had increased to above eighteen hundred and Sunday School attendance was near nine hundred. "We feel that we are still in a stage of preparation for very much greater things," says the pastor.

Taylors Baptist Church, Taylors, South Carolina

From Maryland, our modern Morgan Edwards could travel to upper South Carolina to the small town of Taylors, not far from Greenville. His heart would thrill to what he saw, and he might write in as glowing terms as he used of those he visited two hundred years earlier. Some of the original members of Sandy Creek early made their way to this general region and established a church, as zealous in reaching out as its mother. The church at Taylors is like that early South Carolina forebear.

A few years ago it was a small church in a small town. Then it caught a vision of reaching people. It found a way to involve in Bible study young adults from nearby college and university campuses. When new homes began to dot the area — bedrooms for people who worked in Greenville — the church found ways to reach for Bible study those who lived there. In 1970 the church had grown to 750 in Sunday School attendance; three years later to more than 1,000. E. L. Carswell is the pastor of this church with a fast growing Sunday School.

First Southern Baptist Church, Junction City, Kansas

Morgan Edwards would feel the same spirit working in First Southern Baptist Church, Junction City, Kansas, that he found in Sandy Creek. The Sunday School of this church in 1969 reached an attendance level of 121. Two years later this had increased to 207, but in another two years, 1973, the attendance level rose to above 500. What made the difference? The people began to major on outreach, reaching out to find more people for Bible study and to win them to the Lord Jesus.

First Baptist Church, Dallas, Texas

The largest of Southern Baptist churches, First Baptist Church of Dallas, Texas, where W. A. Criswell is pastor, continues to grow. Although situated in the heart of a large city, this church refused to be driven to the suburbs and continued its Bible teaching, people-reaching mission from its location at the heart of the city. Year-by-year its Sunday School enrollment grows and its attendance grows. In 1970 its average attendance was 5,112. The following year it reached an attendance of 5,520, a gain of approximately 400 people. It also gained in 1972 and 1973. This church continues to reach more people. Its example is inspiring to all others.

Woodland Drive Baptist Church, Visalia, California

A Morgan Edwards of the eighteenth century could not even dream of traveling two thousand miles and more from Philadelphia to visit a church; a modern Edwards could not avoid it. He surely would see Woodland Drive Baptist Church in Visalia, where Norman H. Ford is pastor. This pastor says that his church places a strong emphasis on good Bible teaching and that the church finds more and more people who want to study the Bible. This pastor leads his church to provide such Bible teaching and to reach out for people who need and want it. When Ford became pastor on September 1, 1970, he found a church with sixty in Sunday School attendance. One year later the church had doubled and had reached a Sunday School attendance level of 135. By the following year the attendance level had climbed to 196 and in 1973 attendance reached approximately 250. This church has doubled and re-doubled itself in three years time!

The pastor attributes this growth to four factors: (1) the people have a will to work; (2) the church uses proven principles of growth; (3) reaching adults is emphasized; (4) a strong emphasis is placed upon teaching the Bible. This church expects to keep on reaching more people for Bible study and for Christ.

Amid skyscrapers are the towers of the First Baptist Church of Houston, Texas (lower left and left center).

The wooded area adjacent to the Interstate will be the site of new facilities for the First Baptist Church, Houston.

2

Growing Sunday Schools Reaching People

**First Baptist Church
Houston, Texas and Others**

In beginning my own search for growing Sunday Schools I wrote each of the state convention Sunday School secretaries, explaining my purpose and asking each secretary for a list of the fastest growing Sunday Schools in his convention territory. Most of the secretaries responded. From their answers I formed a preliminary list and used it as a basis from which to work. To the list I added names of other churches as I learned of them and of their growth.

Then I wrote each church asking for information about the Sunday School and enclosing a form which I requested the church to complete and return to me. Here again, most churches responded. A few showed no growth, and some were holding their own with small gains. Most, however, were gaining in Sunday School enrollment and attendance. Some were gaining steadily but slowly, while others were growing more rapidly. Some were increasing in truly astounding fashion.

From a study of the returned forms I learned something immediately: Southern Baptist Sunday Schools are growing. As you read this chapter with its list of churches all with growing Sunday Schools, you, too, will see this to be true.

Not every church is here that should be. Missing some churches is the danger inherent in preparing and publishing a list such as this one. Some I failed to discover; others I missed through error or mistake. I regret missing any church which should be here.

Thinking that a three-year period might more nearly represent continuing growth than a sudden gain in one year, I have tried in each case to show the net gain in Sunday School attendance over the three-year period 1970-1973. In some instances I did not do this, but in most the three-year span is the measuring period.

I have emphasized attendance more than any other single criterion, although I realize that other things matter and matter greatly.

Among these, of course, is excellent Bible teaching. The Bible teaching program of a church exists not to secure numbers as such but to enlist, enroll, and involve persons in effective Bible study. If the Bible is not taught and applied to life, if the read, teach, win, and develop cycle is less than complete, the gathering of great numbers of people serves small purposes.

Look at the list. These churches are among the greatest God has called into being.

First Baptist Church, Houston, Texas

When John R. Bisagno became pastor of this church, he found that attendance had declined over a period of several years until the average had dropped to about 500. In 1970, the first year of Bisagno's pastorate, attendance rose to 869. In 1973 an average of 2,272 were present Sunday by Sunday. Growth for the three years? An average of 528 each year, totaling 1,583 for the three-year period.

First Baptist Church, Jacksonville, Florida

This church has shown a consistent growth pattern for many years, but it has had an increased rate of growth recently. With an average attendance of 1,812 reported in 1970 this church reported 2,707 in 1973. This is an increased attendance of 895 in the three-year period. See chapter 3 for the story of this church.

College Heights Baptist Church, Elyria, Ohio

This church is located in a western suburb of Cleveland, Ohio, about forty miles west of the city itself. In 1970 its attendance was 193. In 1973 its attendance level rose to above 700, a gain of more than 500. On a special high attendance day attendance reached above 1,000. See chapter 4 for the story of this church.

Allapattah Baptist Church, Miami, Florida

Don Manuel is pastor of this church. For a long period of time it was a leading Southern Baptist church in Florida and in the nation. One issue of the old *Sunday School Builder* was devoted wholly to a presentation of the church and its program. Within recent years, however, it gradually lost in attendance. Responding to the challenge of the pastor, the church began to grow again.

Bus ministry is a major factor in Sunday School outreach. This is a typical scene at the Park Avenue Baptist Church, Nashville, Tennessee.

Growth at the Guthrie Baptist Church, Guthrie, Kentucky, is partly due to the bus ministry.

In 1970 its Sunday School attendance was 1,132. Three years later it was reaching for Bible study week by week an average of 1,893. This is a three-year gain of 761.

First Southern Baptist Church, Del City, Oklahoma

Del City is a suburb of Oklahoma City. The First Southern Baptist Church there has had a healthy growth pattern for many years and is still reaching more people for Bible study. In 1970 reported average attendance was 1,519 and in 1973 2,235. In three years the church gained 716.

First Baptist Church, Dallas, Texas

Although this is the largest Southern Baptist Church, First Baptist in Dallas, Texas, continues to reach an increasing number of people for Bible study. In 1970 average attendance stood at 5,112. This climbed to 5,520 in 1971, 5,593 in 1972, and 5,676 in 1973. This is a gain of 664 in a period of three years.

First Baptist Church, Hobbs, New Mexico

"I want to say how thankful I am for an excellent staff," says Bailey E. Smith, pastor of the First Baptist Church of Hobbs, New Mexico. Among his staff are Al Cullum, minister of outreach; Rick Braswell, minister of youth; and S. L. Tate Jr., minister of music. In 1972-73 this church baptized 221 people. On the last Sunday of the church year, September 29, 1973, it had 1,198 in Sunday School, a gain of 640 over the 1970 average attendance of 658.

First Baptist Church, Springdale, Arkansas

"What a fabulous year!" With these words Clifford Palmer, pastor of First Baptist Church, Springdale, Arkansas, described 1973 to his people. He gave statistics: "baptized 143, received by letter 712, net increase in Sunday School enrollment 454, present Sunday School enrollment 1,648." On the Sunday that concluded the year, attendance in Sunday School was 1,009. The previous year on the same Sunday attendance was 862. In 1970 the average attendance had been 448. This church made a net gain in attendance of 561 in the three-year period.

North Phoenix Baptist Church, Phoenix, Arizona

In March, 1970, the North Phoenix Baptist Church of Phoenix, Arizona, for the first time reached 1,000 in Sunday School. It maintained the average for an entire month, a glorious victory. On October 1, 1967, the Sunday School enrollment was 1,146 and average attendance was 443. On October 1, 1968, enrollment had increased to 1,249 and attendance to 512. After an enlargement campaign, the Sunday School grew even faster and in March, 1970, reached 1,000 in attendance. In the months of September and October, 1973, the church averaged 1,650 in Sunday School. From 1967 to 1973 a growth of 1,107. From 1970 to 1973 a growth of 550. Chapter 5 recounts the full story of this church.

Dauphin Way Baptist Church, Mobile, Alabama

In 1970 this church reached a Sunday School enrollment of 3,099 and an average attendance of 1,896. By 1966, however, enrollment had dropped to 2,044 and attendance to 1,103. The trend was reversed beginning in 1967. By 1970 enrollment reached 2,623 and attendance 1,537. Three years later the average attendance had risen to 2,185, a gain in three years of 538. On a high attendance day in 1973 this church had more than 3,000 in attendance. Chapter 6 gives a full story of this church.

First Baptist Church of Center Point, Birmingham, Alabama

"In 1970 we averaged between 850 and 900 in Sunday School. We are now averaging over 1,350 per Sunday a little over two years later," said pastor Ralph D. Feild in a letter in April, 1973. How was the church able to make these gains? The pastor attributes it to: evangelism visitation, deacon visitation, bus outreach and children's worship, and an enthusiastic promotion of the church program. In three years' time this church gained 500 in Sunday School attendance.

Briarlake Baptist Church, Decatur, Georgia

This church is in one of the cities of the metropolitan Atlanta area. From its beginning as a church it has had a steady and consistent growth and maintains the pattern. By 1970 it had reached an attendance average of 963. Three years later, on October 10,

1972, (not a special Sunday) it reached 1,441 in Bible study. This is a gain of 478 in the three-year period. Briarlake keeps on growing, reaching people for Bible study.

First Baptist Church, Wichita Falls, Texas

The pastor of this church, Landrum Leavell, became concerned for the church that it reach more people for Christ. He communicated his concern to his people and they responded. In the three-year period 1970-73 the church increased 422 in Sunday School attendance, from 1,390 to 1,812. The full story of this church is told in chapter 7.

Curtis Baptist Church, Augusta, Georgia

Lawrence Bradley, Jr., has been pastor of this church since 1960. While the church has advanced steadily under his guidance and leadership, growth continues. In the three-year period 1970-73 Sunday School enrollment increased from 2,513 to 3,575 and attendance from 1,023 to 1,445, a gain of 422. See chapter 8 for more about this church.

Tallowood Baptist Church, Houston, Texas

From its birth as a church Tallowood has a history of reaching out for people. The three years 1970-73 saw the church continuing its growth. The Sunday School average attendance in 1970 was 1,382; in 1973 it was 1,798. This is a gain of 416. Lester B. Collins, Jr., is pastor of this church.

Graceland Baptist Church, New Albany, Indiana

"The one most important aspect of the growth of our church has been a church-wide prayer ministry which has undergirded every program started or thought of," says pastor Elvis Marcum of Graceland Baptist Church, New Albany, Indiana. "Through the power of prayer and God's use of dedicated lay people and church staff, a miracle has happened." Statistics do not tell all the story, but they do show something of the extent of the miracle of which the pastor speaks. In 1970 the Sunday School attendance average was 503; this was a gain of 94 over the previous year and of 236 over the previous two years. By the end of 1973 attendance had climbed to over 900, a gain in the three-year period 1970-73 of 400. This is a miracle in itself, but it is a prelude to the victories the church will yet achieve.

Hyde Park Baptist Church, Austin, Texas

From an average attendance in 1970 of 736, this Sunday School reached an average of above 1,100 in 1973, a gain of 400 in the three years. On a special Sunday in March, 1973 an attendance of 1,923 was reached. Ralph M. Smith is pastor of this church.

Mountain Park First Baptist Church, Stone Mountain, Georgia

In 1970, this church, where Gerald E. Bagwell is pastor, reached an average of 220 in Sunday School. In 1973 it reached an attendance level of 614, a gain of 396.

Travis Avenue Baptist Church, Fort Worth, Texas

This church and pastor, James Coggin, found a way to reverse their downward trend and challenged all Southern Baptists to do as they were doing — under the Lord's leadership. In the three years from 1970 through 1973 the church gained in Sunday School attendance from 1,652 to 2,047, an increase of 395. Many other churches, encouraged and enheartened by their example, achieved similar victories.

First Baptist Church, Raytown, Missouri

F. R. Cole is pastor of this church. Sunday School attendance in 1970 was 883, a figure which in itself represented a growth of 36 over the previous year and 47 over the previous two years. In the three years since 1970, however, the church continued its growth at an accelerated rate. Attendance grew to 940 in 1971, to 1,012 in 1972, and reached 1,269 in 1973. Growth for the three-year period: 386. This church inaugurated two Sunday Schools on October 7, 1973.

Horseshoe Drive Baptist Church, Alexandria, Louisiana

"Vision, soul-winning, Bible teaching, enthusiasm, optimism, planning, involvement of people, determination, and leadership — all these anointed by the Holy Spirit constitute the secret of growth at Horeshoe Drive Baptist Church," says pastor Ken Chamblin. Chamblin became pastor in 1968 with the Sunday School attendance averaging about 325. By 1970 attendance had reached 591. Three years later, in mid-1973 the attendance level had gone to 977, a gain in three years of 378.

First Baptist Church, Columbia, South Carolina

During the year 1973 First Baptist Church, Columbia, South Carolina, reached an attendance level of 1,511, a gain of 376 over the previous year. H. Edwin Young is the pastor of this church.

Walnut Street Baptist Church, Louisville, Kentucky

An inner-city church, Walnut Street Baptist Church of Louisville, Kentucky, had suffered some years of decline. Its pastor, Wayne Dehoney, however, believed the church still could and should reach more people for Bible study and for Christ. He challenged the church to go out into the highways and byways and bring them in and led the people in a program implementing this spirit. In the three-year period 1970-73 the average Sunday School attendance gained from 1,200 to 1,555, a total of 355. See chapter 11 for the full story of this church.

First Baptist Church of Ferguson, Ferguson, Missouri

"The spirit of our people is wonderful," says H. G. Willmot, minister of education for this church. In 1970 the church had an average of 533 in Bible study. Three years later, in 1973, attendance had risen to above 900, a gain of 350 in the three-year period. Robert S. Werner is pastor of this church.

Eastwood Baptist Church, Tulsa, Oklahoma

Thomas D. Elliff became pastor of this church in August, 1972. At that time the church had been showing a growth in Sunday School attendance year by year. Average attendance for 1972 was 655, but one year later the Sunday School had reached an attendance level of more than 1,000. This gain of 350 took place in one year's time and created a promise of continued growth. An account of this church is given in chapter 10.

First Southern Baptist Church, Junction City, Kansas

In 1970 the Sunday School of this church showed an average attendance of 149. Three years later with the Sunday School reaching 500 each Sunday, the pastor, R. D. Wooderson, wondered where he would put all the people. He had led the church to set a high attendance goal of 600 and expected to reach it. The major part of this gain occurred in one year's time through the use of a bus ministry. The three-year gain was 350. This church is already mentioned in chapter 1.

Calvary Baptist Church, Clearwater, Florida

Frank Gillham is pastor of the Calvary Baptist Church of Clearwater, Florida. In his weekly bulletin *The Caller* for October 11, 1973, he summarizes three years of growth for the church. Sunday School enrollment grew from 1,088 to 1,608, a gain of 520 in enrollment. Sunday School average attendance gained from 530 to 874, a gain of 344. The attendance level in September and October of the year had risen to more than 900, however, as shown by the weekly reports. This pastor and staff say to the church: "Think outreach."

First Baptist Church, Waco, Texas

"Our growth seems to come because of the Bible-centered and evangelistic pulpit of our pastor. There are growth factors operating also, but the preaching of our pastor has put it together," says Owen Kersh, minister of education for the First Baptist Church of Waco, Texas. This historic church had declined in Sunday School attendance of 604 in 1969, the year Peter McLeod became pastor. By the following year a pattern of growth became evident; Sunday School attendance rose to 729. Three years later, in the fall of 1973, the Sunday School attendance level had risen to 1,050, a gain of 321 in the three-year period.

First Baptist Church, Kenner, Louisiana

From an attendance of 762 in 1970 the First Baptist Church of Kenner, Louisiana increased to an average attendance of 1,067 in 1973. This is a gain of 305.

Glendale Baptist Church, Bowling Green, Kentucky

Richard Oldham, pastor, tells the story of this church: "God has graciously blessed the work at the Glendale Baptist Church using the coupling of five strategic measures to bring us from an enrollment of approximately 1,200 in Sunday School to 1,800 and an increased attendance of nearly 300 over last year at this same time and the winning of 200 precious people to faith in Christ: (1) A major building program — the construction of a $200,000 children's building. (2) promotional features that emphasized high attendance and growing enrollment called "Miracle Day" and "Anniversary Day." On both of these days Sunday School attendance soared for the first time over the 1,000 mark. (3) An enlarged bus ministry seeking to make the Lord's church as close as the street in front of every house in our city. We were greatly challenged in this by the visitation and motivation seminar. (4) A consuming motivation to capture the attention of this city for Jesus Christ and to knock on every door in our city to win the lost for Christ. (5) The building in the minds of our people of an excitement about Sunday School — making it the most profitable study hour of the week for Bible study and soul-winning outreach. We praise God for his blessings."

Dawson Memorial Baptist Church, Birmingham, Alabama

This great church has had many years of steady and consistent growth in reaching more people for Bible study. Its pastor, Edgar M. Arendall, continues to lead the church in outreach. In 1970 its Sunday School attendance average was 1,555. Three years later it had grown to 1,785. This gain of 230 in three years represents the kind of steady growth the church has had over many previous years.

Northwest Baptist Church, Miami, Florida

William Chapman is pastor of this church which has a record of growth from its beginning. In the three years from 1970 through 1973 it increased its Sunday School average attendance from 1,156 to 1,383, an attendance gain of 227.

Redland Baptist Church, Derwood, Maryland

Bob Rich is pastor of this church. The first year he led the church, 1960, the Sunday School averaged 89. The following year Sunday School attendance rose to 117. Three years later attendance had risen to 350, a three-year gain of 232. Dale Higginbotham is minister of youth and music for this church.

Circle Drive Baptist Church, Colorado Springs, Colorado

Lewis Adkinson has been pastor of this church since April, 1968 and during this time the church has shown a consistent pattern of growth. Average Sunday School attendance when he became pastor stood at 270. In 1970 attendance stood at 356. In the fall of 1973 attendance reached 583. In the three-year period 1970-73, the church showed an attendance gain of 227.

First Baptist Church, Paris, Texas

The church bulletin, *The Messenger,* tells the story of the growth of the First Baptist Church of Paris, Texas. "Enrollment gains 500 in three years! Enrollment has moved from 1,641 in 1970 to 2,142 in 1973." This really is a gain of 501. "Attendance increases 220 in 2 years! "Average Sunday School attendance has increased from 795 reported in 1971 to 1,015 for 1973." This is an increase of 110 per year. *The Messenger* also sets a goal for the Sunday School — 2,250 enrolled by January 1, 1974. On a high attendance "Double Miracle Day" in 1973 this church reached 2,042 in attendance. James Semple is pastor of the church.

Seabrook Baptist Church, Seabrook, Maryland

Edwin E. Burris became pastor of the Seabrook Baptist Church of Seabrook, Maryland, on October 1, 1969. The Sunday School average attendance at that time was 203. The following year he led the church to raise its attendance average to 236, but this was only the beginning. In 1973 attendance had risen to 431, a gain in the three years of 215. This church continues to grow, reaching more people for Bible study.

First Baptist Church, Bartlesville, Oklahoma

"A pastor, staff, and people who believe God's business is the biggest and most important thing in the world and treat it as such — this is the most important secret of growth in this church," says Jere Wilson, associate pastor for outreach for the First Baptist Church of Bartlesville, Oklahoma. "Outreach and the Christ-centered life are highly stressed." In 1970 the Sunday School enrollment of this church was 1,749 and attendance average was 783. Three years later the church reached an attendance level above 1,000. On May 6, 1973, a high attendance Sunday saw 1,423, but in September of the same year, without a special high attendance day, 1,458 were present.

First Baptist Church, Monck's Corner, South Carolina

"Oneness of spirit is a most important factor to any growth," says Frank Ling, associate pastor of the First Baptist Church of Monck's Corner, South Carolina. "We have a team of excellent leaders whose sole allegiance is the Lord. Norman E. Gillespie, our pastor, is dedicated and capable and leads in a wonderful way." In 1970 this church had 737 enrolled in its Bible study program and had 322 in regular attendance. Three years later it reached 518 in attendance, an increase of 206. The church weekly bulletin, *First Baptist News,* for October 4, 1973, was headed "Here We Grow Again!" This church will continue to reach more people for Bible study.

First Baptist Church, Whitesburg, Kentucky

First Baptist Church of Whitesburg, Kentucky, grew in enrollment from 405 to 625 in six months' time. In 1970 average Sunday School was 186. In 1973 average attendance reached 386, an increase of 200 in the three-year period. In a 1973 high attendance day a record of 678 was reached. The pastor, Bill Mackey, assigns the basis for this growth to several factors: (1) Foundation, by study of guiding, understanding and administrative books the year before. Pastor and layman attended bus evangelism clinic the month before. (2) Record breaking Sunday, attendance, 512; (3) Lay evangelism school, 65 enrolled, 49 witness, bi-monthly witness visitation continued; (4) Bus added to van and cars; (5) Largest vacation Bible School, 551 over 338; (6) Five-day revival, 53 professions, 401 average attendance; (7) WIN Bible study leaflets and letters and the new member class instrumental in involving new members in new outreach; (8) Two mission Sunday Schools doubled their attendance with visitation and provision transportation.

Putnam City Baptist Church, Oklahoma City, Oklahoma

Putnam City Baptist Church experienced a decline over a number of years. From 1968 through 1972 the Sunday School attendance fell from 912 to 706. Enrollment declined from 2,260 to 1,395. During 1973 the trend was reversed and the attendance once again reached the 900 level — and passed it. The attendance gain was over 200 in this year, with the promise that the new growth pattern will be sustained. Richard B. Douglas is the pastor of this church.

Ninth and O Baptist Church, Louisville, Kentucky

Laverne Butler is pastor of this church. The 1970 record was 835 and the Sunday School reached 1,105 in 1973, a gain of 200.

Middle River Baptist Church, Baltimore, Maryland

Middle River Baptist Church, Baltimore, Maryland, gained about 190 in two years. (See chapter 1 for a short note about this church.) Records for 1970 were not available, but in 1971 the attendance was 672 and in 1973 it was 862. James E. Willey is pastor of this church.

Salem Baptist Church, Columbus, Ohio

The Salem Baptist Church of Columbus, Ohio, began a bus ministry the last Sunday of February, 1972, with a van and five cars. The first Sunday thirty-three riders came. By the following Sunday the church purchased its first bus, prepared it for service and put it on a route. By the fourth Sunday riders had risen to 102 and the church put on a second bus. Sunday School attendance grew from 101 in February, 1972, to 286 in September, 1973, an increase of 185 in seventeen months. James L. Goforth, Sr., is pastor of this growing church.

Woodland Drive Baptist Church, Visalia, California

In 1970 the Sunday School of this church averaged 60 in attendance. In March, 1973, the pastor said: "Last quarter we averaged 234. We are continuing to plan ahead and anticipate an attendance of about 300 this fall. Our expected growth is twenty-five per quarter." This church made a net gain of 178 in three years. (See chapter 1 for words about this church.)

Pacific Beach Baptist Church, San Diego, California

Carl Whitlock is pastor of the Pacific Beach Baptist Church in San Diego. He is leading his church to grow. In 1970 the Sunday School average was 206; in 1973, 375. This is a gain of 169.

Amite Baptist Church, Denham Springs, Louisiana

This is an open country church, located near Baton Rouge. Its area is near suburban. For many years the church has been a strong church and it continues to grow year by year. In 1970 average Sunday School attendance was 385 and in 1973 it had grown to 530, a gain of 145. James K. Pearce is pastor of this church. (See chapter 12 for the full story of this church.)

First Baptist Church, Nashville, Georgia

This church, of which E. Donald Bowick is pastor, gained from 208 to 321 in Sunday School attendance in one year from 1972 to 1973.

Lemon Grove Baptist Church, Lemon Grove, California

This church is one of the many suburban cities which together make up the San Diego metropolitan area. For many years it ran about 200 in Sunday School. Then it was able to increase to about 250. The last several years, however, its growth has been faster. In 1970 it had 831 enrolled and an average in attendance of 431. Three years later, in 1973, its attendance level had risen to 560, a gain over the three year period of 129. This gain is consistent with what the church has done for several years. The church has achieved much of this gain through the use of buses. On a high attendance Sunday in 1973 the church reached over 1,000 in Sunday School. Bob Kleinschmidt is pastor of this church.

Calvary Baptist Church, Chula Vista, California

In the three-year period from 1970 to 1973 the Calvary Baptist Church in Chula Vista, California, gained 115 in Sunday School attendance. In 1970 the Sunday School attendance averaged 98. Its attendance rose to 217 in three years. Bob Seago is pastor.

Ocean View Baptist Church, Norfolk, Virginia

Bus outreach is one of the keys to the growth of the Ocean View Baptist Church of Norfolk, Virginia. The church has six bus routes and reaches about 750 each Sunday in total attendance in its Bible teaching program.

Farmdale Baptist Church, Louisville, Kentucky

Jay Brown is pastor of Farmdale Baptist Church, Louisville, Kentucky. In 1970 the Sunday School enrollment was 733 and attendance averaged 233. The following year enrollment remained the same and attendance increased slightly to 240. The pastor tells the following story of the church. "In October, 1971, the pastor and some other men of the church attended a bus conference. This conference opened up possibilities for Sunday School growth we had never considered before. As a result our church started a bus ministry. The excitement and enthusiasm of this new avenue of evangelism and growth sparked a spirit of new life in our church. We bought three buses and asked Mr. Herman Baumgardner to serve as our bus director. Since the very beginning we have averaged 150 riders on the buses each Sunday.

"Our statistics show a marked increase. In October, 1971, we had 613 enrolled in Sunday School with 233 average attendance. In November, 1972, we had 813 enrolled in Sunday School and 359 average attendance. Our children's worship service has approximately 100 each Sunday. Our church baptized 83 this last associational year and had 67 other additions.

"As a result of the increase in Sunday School and our worship services, we have started five new departments and a children's worship service. Our church is experiencing a perennial revival."

Guthrie Baptist Church, Guthrie, Kentucky

In February, 1972, Guthrie Baptist Church, Guthrie, Kentucky, then without a pastor, had 80 in Sunday School. With hard work and increased enthusiasm the church reached on a special day a peak Sunday School attendance of 200. Later, with a pastor, a second special day was set for October, 1973. At this time an attendance of 224 was reached. Regular attendance climbed to better than 185. Harold Rose is pastor of this church.

First Baptist Church of Heath, Heath, Ohio

"Warm, enthusiastic, involved, motivated membership is the key to our growth," says pastor W. A. Ferguson of the First Baptist Church of Heath in Heath, Ohio. Sunday School attendance grew from 1970 through 1973 from an enrollment of 239 to 450 and from an attendance of 139 to 275, an increase of 136.

Macedonia Baptist Church, Route Three, Bessemer, Alabama

Bobby L. Hadaway is the pastor of this rural church. He tells the story of what happened in the church: "One Wednesday night we had a brainstorming session as to what the people would like to see their church accomplish, both spiritually and materially. Soon, priorities were adopted, such as making the Sunday School the outreach arm of the church. This called for a "People-to-People" consultation with leaders of the state Sunday School department; they were happy to come and help us. We talked about bus outreach. We talked also about an outreach program, about space, and about materials. In short, with the help and guidance of our Sunday School leaders, we put into action the laws of Sunday School growth." Before taking these steps the Sunday School level of attendance in this church was 115; since, attendance has risen to 200 and the pastor looks confidently to the time when it will be much larger still. "Visions without actions are nightmares," he concludes, "but vision with action has God's power."

Kailua Baptist Church, Kailua, Hawaii

Paul Rutledge is pastor of the Kailua Baptist Church and David McQuitty is minister of education and youth. One of the bulletins of this church asks, "Do we really need a new educational building?" and continues: "Just because the nursery's overflowing, and some of the adults meet under the ramp while others meet under the trees, and Sam's class meets in his van, and Dave's class under the stairs? Well," it concludes, "maybe we really don't need another educational building, so long as we never have rain, or any more babies, and if we don't ever, ever grow again." This church is growing within the limits of the space. In 1970 average Sunday School attendance was 165 and in 1973 rose to 243, a gain of 77. The pastor says he searches for ways to provide more space to reach more people. In the meantime "Our people visit. We preach the word of God. God is at work in our midst."

First Baptist Church, Putney, Georgia

In 1970 the Putney Baptist Church reported 209 enrolled in

Sunday School with an average attendance of 104. The Sunday School had been at this level for a number of years. The following year enrollment declined to 179 and attendance to 85. In June, 1971, Johnny R. Boyd became pastor. He led the church to experience a new vision, a new attitude, and an outlook of expectation and hope. One year later enrollment had risen to 288 and attendance to 136. Baptisms increased from 3 to 39. By the close of the year following enrollment rose to 423 and attendance to 279. The church set a goal of "100 more in 74" for each of the four age divisions of the Sunday School. Within two months of the new year the enrollment increase was Adult, 27; Youth, 3; Children, 11; and Preschool, 17. This totaled 58 in two months. From 179 enrolled to 423 indicates a gain of 144; the gain in attendance from 85 to 279 is nearly 200.

Park Avenue Baptist Church, Nashville, Tennessee

This church, where Bob Mowrey is pastor and Bobby Welch is associate pastor, has done an outstanding job of reaching people through a bus ministry and through other ways of outreach. In 1970 the Sunday School had an enrollment of 1,946; in 1973 the enrollment rose to 2,391. This is net gain of 445. In the same period of time the average attendance rose from 945 to 1,602, a gain of 657. During the summer of 1973 this Sunday School reached and maintained an attendance level of more than 2,000. From an attendance average in 1970 of 945 to an attendance three years later of more than 2,000 is the record of truly growing Sunday School.

Highland Avenue Baptist Church, Brooklyn, New York

"The fastest way to find prospects is to knock on doors," says pastor James K. Wright of the Highland Avenue Baptist Church of Brooklyn, New York. When he became pastor of the church in 1967 the church had twenty-five members; sixteen were present for Sunday School the first Sunday. In 1973 the church had more than two hundred present for Bible study Sunday by Sunday. A church can grow in Brooklyn — and it *is* growing.

3

Touching a Growing City by Reaching People

**First Baptist Church
Jacksonville, Florida**

The First Baptist Church of Jacksonville, Florida has a remarkable story. Remarkable for the long continuity of leadership by one pastor, succeeded by his son. Together their service to the church covers thirty-four years. Remarkable for its refusal to leave the downtown, but to continue a ministry to a great city from its central location. Remarkable for its growth, which began the first year Homer Lindsay was pastor and has continued uninterrupted since. Remarkable for the greatly accentuated growth in the present.

In the years 1970-73 the church has grown from a Sunday enrollment of 3,708 to an enrollment of 6,380, from an attendance of 1,814 to an attendance of 3,000. For the five-year period 1968-73 the figures are even more amazing. From an enrollment of 2,600 to 6,380 and from an attendance of 1,250 to 3,000. How has this happened? The two pastors tell the story themselves.

In an address at one of the Sunday School weeks at the Ridgecrest Baptist Conference Center in the summer of 1973, Dr. Homer Lindsay, Sr., spoke of the long relationship of himself and his son, Homer Lindsay, Jr., to the church. "We happen to be a downtown church that is supposed to have died many years ago but we just simply refuse to lie down and die. We believe that God planted the First Baptist Church downtown to minister to all the city of Jacksonville and to all that wish to take advantage of our ministry.

"Thirty-three years ago we adopted as our motto: Always More Than the Year Before. There has never been a year in all this time we have not succeeded in reaching this goal. In Deuteronomy 1:8 God said: 'Behold I have set the land before you: go in and possess the land.' Then he said to Joshua in Joshua 3:5: " 'Sanctify yourselves: for tomorrow the Lord will do wonders among you.'

We have believed this.

"We have had a steady growth through the years, but in the last five years we have had the most fantastic phenomenal growth we have ever experienced.

"Five years ago I announced to the church that I was getting ready to retire and that they should begin to look around for a pastor to succeed me. I told them I would give them enough time, so they appointed a pulpit committee. The committee and the church were led to extend a call to my son to serve as a co-pastor. So for four years we served as co-pastors of the church. My son had had a multiple outreach ministry for seventeen years in Miami. 'Dad, I do not want to do away with anything you have done,' he said to me. 'I want simply to build upon the foundation you have with a multiple outreach.' Our Sunday School enrollment has grown. Our average attendance in Sunday School has increased, and our work has been strengthened. We began a bus ministry in January, 1969, with one bus. Today we have seventeen buses. We have enrolled 1,680 through the ministry, and our buses bring in an average of 600 people Sunday by Sunday."

Homer Lindsay Sr., graduated from the University of Tennessee and Southwestern Baptist Theological Seminary and received a D.D. degree from Union University in Jackson, Tennessee. He has been president of the Tennessee Baptist Convention, the Florida Baptist Convention, vice-president of the Southern Baptist Convention, and served six years as president of the Foreign Mission Board of the Southern Baptist Convention. He has made several trips around the world visiting mission fields.

Homer Lindsay, Jr., is a graduate of Stetson University and Southwestern Baptist Theological Seminary. He received the Doctor of Ministries degree from Luther Rice Seminary, Jacksonville, Florida. He wrote his doctoral thesis on "How to Build an Evangelistic Church." He was pastor of Northwest Baptist Church in Miami for sixteen years. There he developed a work from a mission of 42 to a church of 3,800 members. He has served six years on the Board of Baptist Bible Institute, Graceville, Florida, and ten years on the Board of Southwestern Baptist Theological Seminary. He came to the First Baptist Church of Jacksonville in 1968, first as co-pastor and upon the retirement of his father in 1972, as pastor.

The younger man continues to lead the church, building upon the work done by his father.

The father explains the growth of the church as due to hard work in applying the formula for Sunday School growth developed by Arthur Flake, pioneer Southern Baptist Sunday School leader.

"When I was a young pastor starting out I came under the influence of W. D. Hudgins, then state Sunday School secretary in Tennessee," he says. This great leader used to say that the way to build a Sunday School was to find them, fetch them, and fix them. As you recognize this is a short statement of the method commonly called Flake's Formula for Sunday School growth. Its complete statement has five ideas: (1) locate the prospects, (2) enlarge the organization, (3) enlist and train the workers, (4) provide the space, and (5) go after the people. This formula planted itself in my mind," Lindsay's eyes twinkled. "You know, it works. Nothing has changed about the Sunday School program in these years except working it. If it's worked, the basic Sunday School program we had thirty years ago is just as good and sound today as it has ever been.

"Nothing works itself, however; there is no magic. I suppose the most unpleasant word in the English language is the word *work;* yet there is no other way to build a great Sunday School. There's no way to reach people except to work at the job.

In the thirty-three years that I have been in Jacksonville, it's been line upon line, precept upon precept, laying one brick upon another brick upon another brick, working at it day and night, in season and out of season, all the time speaking to the fundamental Southern Baptist methods. When everyone was excited and frantic, going here and there, we never departed from these methods. We stayed with them, and God has blessed us in a most wonderful and phenomenal way."

The younger Lindsay reiterates and reinforces what his father says. He states as a conviction that the mandate of the church is to make disciples. "I feel the priority of the church is the disciple-making business," he says. As he talks about the church, his conversation relates to finding prospects, a program of visitation, an emphasis upon evangelism, the proclamation of the Word, and the development of the saved into mature witnessing disciples.

Locating Prospects in a Large City

To discover prospects in Jacksonville, a city of 500,000 people, the church promotes a Saturday teenage visitation. It meets for thirteen weeks in the fall and eight weeks in the spring, not the year round. This visitation actually is a prospect discovery effort. This past fall the project averaged approximately 150 teenagers participating each Saturday. The teenagers meet the pastor at the church at 10 A.M. He organizes them into teams and they go out on three buses to visit two-by-two doing survey work. Each team visits approximately 50 houses on a Saturday.

To keep this prospect discovery program functioning requires the work of a full-time secretary. This worker plans the visitation, preparing for each team a small map of the area to be surveyed, and securing it to a clipboard. She also prepares an envelope containing pencils and literature to leave in homes visited. The pieces are four-color; they cost approximately four cents each.

On the clipboard are family prospect cards. The visitors fill out a card for each family not attending church anywhere. If the family attends or is involved anywhere, no card is filled out.

This People Search by its youth is the major source of church prospects. Each weekly effort produces about 450 new prospects. During the periods these youth are visiting, the prospect file quickly grows large.

Another means of securing prospects is through a telephone ministry. This ministry is manned by about fifty women who concentrate on apartment complexes. They telephone a number and keep telephoning until they receive an answer. Most of those contacted are couples. The telephone visitor secures the information. If the couple is not attending anywhere, the church mails a brochure — the same the teenagers leave in homes they visit.

Visiting Prospects

Adult classes and other departments are organized with outreach leaders. The weaker classes have two outreach leaders. Classes are organized with group leaders also.

The church has a regular organized visitation day — Tuesday is the visitation day. The ladies meet on Tuesday morning. Presently they average between 125 and 140 present and visiting on

Tuesday mornings. Men meet at 5:30 on Tuesday evening. They have supper together — with music and testimonies before they go out visiting. Presently the men average about 175 men on Tuesday evenings. This year the church goal is to average 200 men and 150 ladies at the two visitations.

Bus teams or "missionaries" have their visitation on Saturday morning. They gather at 9:00 for a brief promotional meeting, then go out to visit their riders and to search for new riders.

Since people drive anywhere from six to twelve miles to attend, the church feels it important to provide maps — we therefore have maps of the expressway systems and the downtown area, showing the church parking lots. In the visit in the home one of the important areas of the visit is an explanation of the map, pointing out how the prospect can get downtown and to the church.

"We feel it's important in our visits to commit the people we are visiting and we urge our people to commit them in the home to attend one of the services," says Lindsay.

Welcoming Visitors

Since downtown churches have the reputation of being cold, indifferent, and unfriendly, the church makes a positive effort to break this, to create a feeling of warmth and welcome so that people find it on their first visit.

Deacons work the parking lots on Sunday morning. As the people drive down we have set out sandwich boards pointing out the parking lots. When people pull into the parking lots, the deacons assist them to park and then show them where the classification area is. Some twenty people work the classification area. They assist in filling out the registration forms and take the members of the family to the departments they will be attending.

In the department, someone is assigned to the couple. This person introduces the couple to others and after Sunday School is over assists them in getting the children, goes to church with them, sits by them, and introduces them to still other people. After the service, they introduce the couple to the pastor. If there are nursery children, they go to the nursery with them, and then return to the parking lot where their car is parked. The church feels that this kind of kindness and consideration has much to do with the success of the work also.

Enrolling People in Bible Study

Bible Study has a priority position. "You don't come three Sundays to get to be a member of our Sunday School," says Homer Lindsay, Sr. "You are enrolled the first Sunday you come, if you are willing to be enrolled. And we enroll all church members in Sunday School. In 1958 we began enrolling all church members. When you join the church, you immediately become a part of our Sunday School. Your name is put in the weekly paper and you are assigned to a class and department. And it has worked! We've never had any problem with it at all, and so when you join the First Baptist Church you join the Sunday School."

Due to a special concentration of effort on reaching young couples, the church has over a thousand young couples enrolled in Sunday School. These are in the twenty-five to thirty-five age bracket. This is an area that is largely unreached in many places. The concentrated efforts on seeking to reach them for Bible study carries with it great rewards.

The bus Sunday School is separated from the regular Sunday School. The bus Sunday School meets from 10:45 to 12:00. They utilize one of the educational buildings that had been previously utilized from 9:30 to 10:30 by the regular Sunday School.

On Sunday night in order for us to care for the crowds, it is necessary for us to have several children's worship services. We take care of about four hundred children through the sixth grade on Sunday night in order for us to be able to accommodate the people that attend. Last night we had over fourteen hundred in our training program and are averaging presently about fifteen hundred in the worship service. That is, the worship service and the children's services combined.

Bible Exposition from the Pulpit

The pastor feels that his style and type of preaching also has something to do with the Lord's blessings upon the church. "I use the expository type preaching," he says.

"I take the people through one book of the Bible on Sunday

The First Baptist Church, Jacksonville, Florida, on a Sunday morning.

morning, another book of the Bible on Sunday night, and still another on Wednesday night. The people respond to this type of Bible teaching and seldom is anyone in one of the services seen without a Bible. They not only open their Bibles and use them, but many of them take notes as we go through the study. This emphasis on the study of God's Word, along with an emphasis on Christ and on evangelism and an involvement of the people and outreach has produced an exuberantly happy congregation.

"People, when they visit our church, are constantly amazed by the wonderful spirit, the spirit of love, and the spirit of excitement that permeates the entire church life. They often ask what is responsible for that wonderful experience. I feel, of course, that there are several things that are responsible, but I feel that primarily it is that we have such a large number of people involved in outreach, and because we do, we're having so many people saved. The excitement is people who are involved in reaching people and people who are being reached and coming into the church as new Christians who are excited about the Lord and the things of the Lord."

The Wednesday Evening Services

Wednesday evening is an important time at the church. As already mentioned, the pastor brings the same kind of verse-by-verse Bible exposition he brings at the Sunday services. He credits this as largely responsible for the strong Wednesday service.

"The Wednesday evening service has about 1,100 in attendance," he says. "We use our graded choir program to undergird our Wednesday evening service. All of our graded choirs with the exception of the adults robe out for the service on Wednesday evening. The senior high choir serves as the service choir sitting in the choir loft. The others robe out and sit in different sections of the auditorium. They do not all sing each week. The senior high choir sings each week, but the other choirs rotate in singing with the smaller choirs only singing occasionally. This has helped to undergird this service."

Emphasis on Evangelism

The Sunday School is positively evangelistic and the evangelistic spirit permeates the entire program of the church.

The church has about fifty counselors. These are men and women who have been trained to counsel those who walk the aisles making decisions. We present to the church and vote on those who respond. Then everyone, no matter what the decision made, goes to the counseling room. There each one is dealt with personally. In the counseling room we commit them to attend the new member class. A strong effort is made to enlist every new member in the new church member class. Mrs. Homer Lindsay, Sr., has been teaching the new member class for twenty-five years. She still is teaching this class. This is the only job she has in the church, and she stays right on top of it. She goes and visits the new members, she calls them, and she writes them cards and letters when they miss. A large percentage of the new members complete a six-week long class. After the completion of this class, new members are led into a four-week class in which they are instructed in how to witness. The church offers each new member a total of ten weeks help and instruction.

The church emphasis in the spring, February, March, and April, is called Operation Andrew. This is an effort throughout the entire Sunday School to reach new people and enroll new people in Bible study. This has been a very important phase of the work and year by year achievers marked results.

The Vacation Bible School is held in June. Although the downtown situation makes Vacation Bible School difficult, the church enrolled twenty-five hundred in Bible School and saw over three hundred saved in the summer of 1973.

Advertising

The church believes in advertising. It has a radio ministry, being on the radio each day for a total of thirteen times a week. It uses billboards, having space on every main expressway in the city. It also makes extensive use of the newspapers to display advertising of the services on the church page each Saturday. The several visitation efforts have distributed several hundred thousand four-color folders telling about the church.

Excitement — a Key Word

Excitement has permeated the entire church life. From the oldest members down through the youth is this true. A large group of dedicated young people, college and high school age, live for Christ day-by-day. Twenty-eight young men in the last eighteen months have responded to the call of the gospel ministry and are studying in college — not to be preachers but to be better preachers.

One of the thrilling aspects of the organized visitation is to see the large number of older people who are involved, both in the ladies' and the mens' visitation efforts. The thrill is heightened by seeing them involved along with the younger people.

The Future of the Church

The church is now making plans to build a five million dollar auditorium that will seat 3,400 people. Our goal last year was 6,000 enrolled in Sunday School, and our Sunday School increased last year from 5,000 to slightly over 6,000. Our goal for 1974 is 7,000 enrolled in Sunday School. With 7,000 enrolled in Sunday School we will have an average attendance of approximately 3,500. "Presently, we are not able to care for that many people, the pastor admits. "But we have bought some adjoining property that has some buildings on it. One is a large funeral home, and we have placed our Senior High Department in this former funeral home. This department, the tenth, eleventh, and twelfth graders are running about 200 in attendance."

Church Spirit

Dr. Homer Lindsay, Sr., concludes with a few words about church spirit. "I have a feeling that the greatest capitol stocks any church has is not its buildings or its equipment. Not these at all. It is the spirit of the church. The compassion of the people; their spirit of love one for another. People are hungry for love and when the spirit of love is present there is a sweet, sweet spirit in any church. People who are hungry, people who are lonely, people who are seeking fellowship will come again and again.

"Forty-seven years I've been preaching," the older of this father-son team adds, "and I'm more excited now than I've ever been, I wish I had forty-seven years more. I think there has never been a time as thrilling and exciting to preach the Word of God and to teach the Word of God as today. I believe people never have been more hungry for the Word of God. When Sunday School teachers prepare well and when they actually expound the Scriptures, and when they lead people in Bible learning, the people return again and again."

First Baptist Church, Jacksonville, Florida, is a downtown church which chose to grow not to die; it is a church that chose to minister to all of the city; it is a church that is touching a growing city by reaching people.

Like father, like son. Homer G. Lindsay, Sr., and Homer G. Lindsay, Jr.

4

Creating a New Day
for Reaching People

Dauphin Way Baptist Church
Mobile, Alabama

Dauphin Way Baptist Church in Mobile, Alabama, might be called a church of the inner city or a church in a changing neighborhood. Either would be corret. It is located in what once was a substantial neighborhood on the fringe of the downtown Mobile area. This location may have contributed to its growth and development into a strong church many years ago. With a strong program it became the largest Southern Baptist Church, if indeed not the strongest of any denomination, in the state of Alabama. Great preachers served as its pastors, men known nationwide as unsurpassed pulpiteers. The buildings were what would be expected for such a church, spacious auditorium or sanctuary, adequate educational facilities, and all located on an entire city block. For an earlier time, parking would have been more than demanded. All was surrounded with spacious lawns.

Then came changes. Some of the same conditions which helped Dauphin Way grow into greatness began to contribute to its decline. The city of Mobile began to grow rapidly, almost unbelievably, always away from Dauphin Way. This would be true of any church near the heart of a growing city, but especially true in Mobile. This city spreads along a shoreline where several great rivers join themselves to create Mobile Bay. The old downtown sits on the west bank, Dauphin Way stands at the outer edge of the old downtown. To the north, to the south, and to the west, Mobile could grow — and did — with each newly developed area or suburb taking Dauphin Way people farther from their church, at first a trickle but finally a stream. The stately homes which sourrounded the church became offices for doctors, for lawyers, for insurance agencies, and for many other enterprises. Some were divided into apartments. But those who lived in these apartments failed to see Dauphin Way as they passed coming and going.

Did all this effect Dauphin Way? Yes. The Sunday School began to lose in attendance. Then Sunday School enrollment dropped down. Church membership declined. The loss became pronounced and for six consecutive years gained momentum.

At its peak Sunday School enrollment had reached 3,100; in these six years it dropped to less than 2,000. Attendance once had come up to an average of 1,869 for an entire year. That year, 1960, saw many Sundays with more than 1,900 present. But no more. After six years of loss, Sundays now saw an attendance as low as seven or eight hundred.

While seven hundred would seem tremendous to a church which a few years earlier had reached only three or four hundred, it suggested something quite different to one that had seen twice that many each week. Where would it end?

At this point in the life of the church Jaroy Weber became pastor. A native of Louisiana, Weber was a graduate of Louisiana College and had been pastor of the First Baptist Church in West Monroe, Louisiana and later director of evangelism for the Louisiana Baptist Convention. He returned to the pastorate and came to Dauphin Way from the First Baptist Church of Beaumont, Texas.

Among the questions he might have asked — or which might have been asked him — as he came to the church, many concerned the very survival of Dauphin Way. How long can a church exist when it continues to lose a hundred people in Sunday School attendance every year? Must a church near the heart of a city always lose members when the members move to the suburbs? Must a church in an older part of a city become content with reaching and ministering to a limited number of people only? "Can those whom Dauphin has lost and is losing be regained?" "Can they be led to come the long distances from where they now live?"

To at least some of these questions the new pastor received only pessimistic answers. Many people, even some still intensely loyal to the church, had little faith in its future. But not all. Some of those who had stayed with the church believed God still had great things for it. "Because of the rich heritage of this church, it needs to live," they said. "And because of doors of opportunity waiting to be opened if we can discover the keys." Their answers were moved with hope and expectation.

Sensing the need of a serious review of the church's total ministry, especially as related to outreach, the people responded to an appeal by the pastor to face the situation calmly and realistically. What is it? How can we meet it? What is the place of this church in our city? In an attitude of prayer, of concern, and, yes, of anticipation as well, the church appointed a ten-member committee to study the past, the present, and the future of the Dauphin Way congregation.

One thing immediately became apparent: a "business as usual" approach was not and could not get the job done in Mobile's dynamic and rapidly changing society. To maintain the status quo was to be left behind. It was to relegate the church to an increasingly limited and ineffective ministry. To move ahead, then, was the only way. To this consideration the committee turned its attention.

Out of its study the committee made several recommendations. The first was that the church come to a positive decision to remain in its present location, rejecting and abandoning any idea of relocating, and that it do whatever was necessary to get the people to come there to church.

The second, and in many ways the most important of all the recommendations of the committee, was that the church place itself in the "people reaching" business. This called for making a commitment to reach people for Bible study and for Christ and for making this the first priority for the church. To these first two recommendations the church agreed wholeheartedly.

The committee also asked the church to make studies searching for needs and then devise plans for meeting these needs once they were identified. Finally the committee proposed a twenty-year, five million dollar building program to include five new buildings and also the purchase of additional property. This would provide when completed a spacious religious campus to minister to any and every person under any and all circumstances. The plan would be carried out in phases or stages.

When this final recommendation was adopted unanimously by the church, the action was big news. It made the front page headlines of the city newspapers.

Not that the city was not conscious already of changes taking place at Dauphin Way. For months, to let the city know it had not died, the church had been using a catchy slogan, "A New Day at Dauphin Way." By itself the slogan told the story, and the church used every possible way to get it before the people, including night-lighted billboards on major thoroughfares and display newspaper advertisements.

The people began to return to Dauphin Way. Some with new confidence in its ability to achieve for Christ's kingdom and some out of curiosity to see what really was happening. At first the return was no more than trickle, but it promised greater things would happen.

What has happened since then? This question is answered in part by a headline which appeared in "The Dauphin Way Baptist," the church weekly mail-out bulletin to its members and friends. The issue is dated March 23, 1973, and says, "March 25 — Greatest Day at Dauphin Way." The headline screams for attention. What was that greatest day? The day the Sunday School goal for attendance was set for 3,000. The Sunday School reached that goal.

Of course, it was a special day, but earlier there were no special days. Before the special day attendance had been pushing 2,000; after the special day, many Sundays saw an attendance of more than 2,000. Five months later, on a second special day the attendance once again zoomed over 3,000.

What did Dauphin Way do to make so dramatic a turnaround? Surely it's not easy for a church to make an about face. Could other churches follow the lead of Dauphin Way if its actions were identified? Can we know them. The answer to each of these questions is yes.

Leadership

Leadership often is the key to the success or failure of a church, and leadership always spells the difference between churches. This includes, but is not confined to the pastoral leadership. Staff members and also officers and teachers of a Sunday School are parts of the leadership team. The actions and attitudes of each and every team member is important and vital to success.

In the case of Dauphin Way, the first leader was and is Jaroy Weber, the pastor. It was he who led the church to evaluate its ministry, envision its possibilities, and set some priorities to make reaching more people possible.

He also acted to bring together a staff of people, each highly qualified as a leader in his or her respective area. Having brought them, he freed them to do the work of which they were capable.

The first of these was James Neyland. Neyland had worked with the pastor in a former pastorate; they knew each other and worked well together. Neyland shares his pastor's concern for evangelism and tremendous ability in guiding the development of an outreaching educational program for a church.

As the staff grew, care was exercised that each staff member, like Neyland, share the pastor's concern for the church and its ministry.

Involving the church in self-evaluation was an early achievement of its leadership. Evaluation is not as favorite a word with Southern Baptists as it might be, yet Dauphin Way looked critically at itself. Seeing a vision and transmitting that vision to others always is an achievement of leadership; this the leaders of Dauphin Way also were able to do. Out of the leadership team was born the vision of the "new day" and later the "greatest day." Working successfully to translate dreams into work and from work into reality is leadership's ultimate accomplishment.

Witnessing

The keynote of the ministry of Dauphin Way is witnessing, sharing Christ with those who do not know him. The pastor considers the turning point of the church to have come when "several of us decided that while we might not do a lot of things, two things we could and would do: witness ourselves and teach some of our people how to share Christ with others."

A training program for soul-winners was instituted which resulted in a few discovering the joy of helping a person to be saved. The church moved into a continuous witnessing, training, and activities approach, meeting for training on Sunday and Thursday evenings and going out actually to witness on Thursday.

Subsequently, they added a full-time minister of evangelism to the staff to lead this area of work and to direct the training program. The church also developed its own set of materials, using the pattern of the WIN materials of the Sunday School Board. Jimmy Andrews served as minister of evangelism until November, 1973.

The spirit of witnessing permeates the entire life of the church. The minister of education assigns an emphasis upon evangelism as one of the secrets of a growing Sunday School and uses the outreach thrust of the Sunday School not only to enroll more people, but to open doors for witnessing. The Sunday School workers understand their task as enrolling the unsaved and then witnessing to them at each and every opportunity.

Witnessing is the key to the tremendous success of Dauphin Way in reaching youth. "Our youth are geared to witness, at school or wherever they are," says Dennis Wood, then minister of youth. "Many of them are involved in our bus ministry. They are out every Saturday morning, visiting and are back on Sunday morning to ride the buses." Some of the youth have been through four or five witness-training courses. However, they not only train; they also witness.

The witnessing thrust of the Sunday School is brilliantly evident in the bus outreach program. Many children have been won to Christ after having come to Sunday School first on a bus, but countless adults have been reached and won because of the concern shown for the children.

Evangelism is the heartbeat of Dauphin Way; no matter how a person first comes in contact with the church, someone soon will share Christ with him.

Enlargement

A third factor in the growth of Dauphin Way's Sunday School is the regular and periodic addition of teaching units. The minister of education acknowledges that he uses the classic Flake Formula for Sunday School growth, of which one of the five points is: Enlarge the organization. In an address at the Glorieta Baptist Conference Center in the summer of 1973, Neyland suggested planning each year the number of new departments and classes to be organized and setting this up at the beginning of the Sunday School year insofar as possible. Of course this does not preclude the addition of units from time to time during the year as needed.

"We started four new organizational units in 1968," Neyland says. "In 1969 we started six new departments, began an appreciable number of new classes, and made adjustment in the total number of workers so we could staff these units." The first of these two years the Sunday School made a new gain in enrollment of 101; the second year the increase was a healthy 469.

In 1971-72 the Children's World was opened. This new facility provided space to begin twelve new departments, an enlargement which called for 110 new workers. The enrollment increase in the Sunday School that year was 815.

The enrollment increases year by year result from positive planning by the minister of education and Sunday School council. Age division by age division, and department by department, the Sunday School is studied and evaluated. The classes also are studied. Where unmet needs are spotlighted, consideration is given to the possibility of creating a unit to meet the needs. New departments and classes added at the beginning of the 1973-74 year causes an expectation of continued growth.

This kind of enlargement calls for a constant enlistment of new workers. When these workers are enlisted the minister of education or the Sunday School director enlist them personally. Before making the decision to invite someone to serve, they study his record of Sunday School participation, not just attendance.

The Sunday School at the beginning of the 1973-74 year had 435 teachers and officers and an enrollment of well over 4,000. The Adult division of the Sunday School has more than 2,000 enrolled and continues to grow. The Sunday School boasts of twelve departments in the Youth Division. Because of the middle-school approach used by the Mobile school system, sixth graders are included here.

The Children's and Preschool division are housed in the new Children's World, a complex of seven buildings located across a street from the main church property. These buildings, which include a gymnasium, became available to the church when the girls' school which owned them decided to relocate. The acquisition of these buildings made possible a tremendous expansion of the children's work, the creation of the new departments mentioned above. Over 1,100 children, schools grades 1 through 5 now are enrolled in the departments of this division.

Without a constantly enlarging organization the Dauphin Way Sunday School never could have reached the large number of people now touched by its ministry. Will it continue to enlarge its organization? Yes, because its leadership and its people know that this is necessary if the mission of the church is to be realized.

Bus Outreach

To understand fully the miracles of outreach which have taken place in the Dauphin Way Sunday School the past several years one must look at the bus outreach program. Look at those who are involved in the ministry; look at the people they reach; look at the teaching they receive and the concern showered upon them; but most of all look at the changes taking place in the lives of people. "Through the bus outreach program missions become real to me," says one church member. "There was a time when missions was something vague to which I was happy to give my money and happy for the church to have a part in. Now that has all changed. I still want to give my money, even more than before. I still want my church to participate through the Cooperative Program, even more than before. But missions is also what I do on Saturday and Sunday and many other days in the week through my involvement with people through bus outreach. It has changed my life."

The church first bought a couple of old buses to use for short trips of various kinds. Later, two or three men of the church heard about some of the things happening in other churches and started out one Saturday. Only one person rode the bus the following day, but enough had been done to cause the church to desire to go ahead. The pastor and minister of education led the church to add a part-time bus director to the staff.

At the pastor's suggestion, this new staff member visited a large church already having real success in bus outreach. Within a month the program was underway with two buses. This time the buses began to fill and another was added. Then another. And another. When buses were running, the church made the bus minister a full time staff position. Now it runs seventeen buses.

On a given Sunday from six to seven hundred people will ride the buses. Mr. Neyland explains some of the problems connected with the bus program. "We started bringing the children into the regular departments," he says. "This worked fine at first, but the departments soon got too large. Then we decided to have two

Sunday Schools for children. The children who rode the buses attended worship during the regular Sunday School time, then they had Sunday School during the regular morning worship hour.

"This worked fine except for getting enough workers. Also, many of our people were afraid this gave the appearance that we were making second-class church members and Sunday School members of those who rode our buses. When the buildings became available and our Children's World came into being, we were able to create enough departments so that we could go back to one Sunday School for all our children."

About half the children who attend the Sunday School ride buses and about half come with parents. On the buses are children from the finest sections of the city and also children from welfare homes. "All of these are just children as the other children go," says Neyland.

In addition to the Sunday morning use of the buses, there is an extensive bus ministry throughout the week, including transportation for senior citizens and transportation for other church activities.

Planning

Both Jaroy Weber and James Neyland believe one of the secrets of a growing Sunday School is planning.

The center of the Sunday School planning process for Dauphin Way is the Wednesday night meeting of the teachers and officers.

Prior to this meeting, however, is a meeting with the directors. This meeting is each Sunday evening. One of the commitments each of the sixty-three directors makes when enlisted is to be present regularly for this meeting. The meeting is most important. About half the time is spent talking about and working with the Sunday School as a whole. Not as much time is spent talking about problems as in presenting plans for work to be done. The directors then carry the plans back to their workers and gain cooperation.

After the general period, the division directors, all of whom are paid staff members, meet with the directors of their several divisions. There they discuss the promotion of plans, training efforts, teaching needs, and anything else that is needed.

Then on Wednesday night, the directors meet with their departments to plan how to carry out all that has been agreed upon in the Sunday evening council. The department directors also use part of the Wednesday night time for developing the outreach thrust of the department and for the promotion of better Bible teaching in the classes.

The bus workers, about sixty of them, also meet on Wednesday night at the same time as the other Sunday School workers. The bus director has an outline of study that he follows. He meets about thirty minutes with his bus captains, and then all the workers meet together. They talk about what they hope to do, set goals, and make plans for reaching their goals. Later, on Saturday morning when they meet to visit, they use the goals as guides and motivators for their work. On Saturdays some visit riders, and other survey for future enlistment.

Better Bible Teaching

Dauphin Way believes in better Bible teaching for all ages. "We feel that when we bring people here, the word of God must be taught," the pastor declares. Jim Neyland and the staff member division directors agree.

The Wednesday night teachers and officers' meeting functions to create a desire for an upgrading of teaching and also furnishes immediate help for the teacher's Sunday by Sunday work. In addition the church offers teachers sixteen hours of training during the course of the year. Four seminars and other special training events also are offered.

Sunday School department directors are expected to use their influence as best they can to improve the quality of teaching in their departments. This they do by visiting the classes and then by using the teaching improvement period of the Wednesday night meeting.

The teachers are willing to try different methods; they are also willing to use the older methods when they can use them effectively.

Big Days

Dauphin Way uses big days to boost enthusiasm, lend encouragement, to the people, and keep spiritual excitement at a high plane. "Reaching the attendance goal on a big day is important and we work hard to reach it," the pastor says. "But, really that is not the main objective. We see this as a step in our effort to increase our momentum in reaching people."

The big day also affords opportunity for creating a flow of favorable publicity. The promotion of the day increases the ways in which the name of the church can be kept before the people. The publicity pieces go into more homes and touch more people than the week-by-week promotion efforts of the church.

How are plans for a big day at Dauphin Way formulated and developed? Not by the pastor and his staff alone. The idea first is presented to the directors. It is talked about there. The goal and its possible size are discussed freely. Then the directors talk to their departments. The classes and departments may set individual goals and then the overall goal is determined. While this process may not be followed exactly each time, the department directors and the workers in the departments always are involved in goal setting.

A special promotion committee may be appointed to work on goal promotion. In the big day in October, 1973, the mainline promotion plan was simply to get every possible person to sign a pledge card to be present on the high attendance Sunday. The principal hope for success was an intensified visitation using the pledge cards. At another big day a different approach altogether may be used.

Dauphin Way does not depend upon big days to provide the enthusiasm and excitement the Sunday School needs. These are generated by the week-to-week program of good Bible teaching. The big day simply focuses upon visitation and victory for one Sunday above others.

Buildings

"The building sets the pattern," stated J. N. Barnette, great Sunday School leader of twenty-five years ago in his memorable book *The Pull of the People*. Dauphin Way wisely has provided the buildings necessary for growth and will build more as need continues.

One of these buildings is the Christian Life Center. It is a recreation center, but leaders insist it is far more. Bill McIlwain, recreation director describes it as existing for two purposes: (1) to provide a center for all-around recreation and leisuretime activities for entire families; and (2) to be used in an outreach ministry to draw people to the church, to get them interested in the activities, and to provide opportunities for witnessing. The Christian Life Center was opened in February, 1970. The fellowship and spirit of closeness it promotes among the people is a definite asset to a growing Sunday School not to mention the addition of the space to Bible teaching areas.

Children's World, already described, also provided space when needs were great. Because of the additional space, growth became possible. Some children's workers came to the Children's World buildings at a seeming sacrifice. Their places of work in the older buildings had been better kept and more beautiful, in some cases even arranged better. Yet, the school buildings in Children's World began to take shape and the teachers cooperated wonderfully. And the children's departments grew.

Spirit

Perhaps the greatest thing about the Dauphin Way Baptist Church is its spirit. While definition may be impossible, the failure to recognize the presence of a glowing spirit also is impossible. Dauphin Way has a spirit of dedication and of commitment. It also has a warm spirit of fellowship. Above all, it has a spirit of reaching out to any person who needs Jesus to share the gospel with him. If the difference in churches is spirit, it is easy to understand why Dauphin Way was able to turn around and enter into a "new day."

Perhaps the most significant thing about the story of Dauphin Way is the hope it gives to any church that is slipping in enrollment, attendance, and in other ways. Not many churches are as large as Dauphin Way, yet spirit does not depend upon size. Nor do all the things Dauphin Way did depend upon size. Nor does the gift of the Spirit of God depend upon size. Any church can commit itself to reaching people. No matter what size, any church can set priorities of evangelism and better Bible teaching. Any church that truly seeks it, also can have a new day, its own "new day."

On December 3, 1973, Dr. Weber became pastor of the First Baptist Church of Lubbock, Texas. In his letter to the Dauphin Way Church he expressed his love for the people and his expectation of even greater victories for the church.

DEAR FRIENDS:

On August 14, 1966, I accepted the call to become your pastor at Dauphin Way Baptist Church and today I face another momentous decision. I feel that God has led in this decision; therefore, I offer my resignation as pastor of your great church to accept the call of the First Baptist Church of Lubbock, Texas, to become effective December 3, 1973.

Let me assure you that I have thrown up every possible barrier to test the will of God and he has overcome every one of them. To be honest with you, in light of what has happened, I have no other option but to go, and not to do so would cause me to face the possibility of being out of God's will. My only reason for going is to do the will of God.

This being God's will I know he has great plans for you in his future. I would not do anything to hurt this work where I have given seven years of my life. I appeal to you to join in putting your shoulder to the task and support the work in every area.

You have more potential for growth than at anytime in many years. Facilities, finances, and fellowship of Dauphin Way is at an all time high. It would sadden me to have you fail in keeping on in this ministry. I appeal to you to stick together and undergird your new pastor with the same love and loyalty you gave to me.

These next few days will be deeply emotional for us all. Let us not make it sad days but glad days as we give thanks to God for all he has done in this ministry and what he is going to do.

I thank God for your patience with me in my weaknesses, your forgiveness in my mistakes, and your confidence in my decision to reach this city for Christ. I shall always praise your greatness, pray for your fellowship, and preach the Bible as the Word of God.

Permit me to quote a friend, as Steerforth said in his last message to David Copperfield, "Always remember me when I was at my best."

Sincerely,

JAROY WEBER

5

Developing Aggressiveness in Reaching People

College Heights Baptist Church
Elyria, Ohio

College Heights Baptist Church, Elyria, Ohio, began on October 16, 1966, when Maurice Mosely, his wife, and their three children met in a union hall for Sunday School and worship. The union hall that Sunday morning was a mess; there had been a party there the evening before. Beer cans were strewn everywhere. Cigarette stubs were ground into the floor. The stench was overpowering.

The preacher and his family cleaned up the hall and then had the first Bible study session and the first worship service — just the five of them. They also committed themselves to reaching the town of Elyria for Bible study and for Christ. At that time the small city, seventy-five thousand population, on the western rim of the Cleveland metropolitan area, had no Southern Baptist witness of any kind.

The young pastor — then twenty-nine years of age — was a recent graduate of the Southwestern Baptist Theological Seminary. A native of Missouri, he was also a graduate of Southwest Baptist College in Bolivar, Missouri, and of Howard Payne College in Brownwood, Texas. He had served as pastor in Oklahoma and in Texas. These experiences helped prepare him for the work in a new field, but of equal — if not greater — importance was the depth of his commitment and of his dependence upon God for guidance and strength. These commitments were shared by his wife and by his children, insofar as they then could understand. The Home Mission Board of the Southern Baptist Convention also provided $500 a month in pastoral support.

In October, 1973, the church observed its seventh anniversary. That month the Sunday School averaged 740 in attendance. One of the Sundays was a record-breaking day with 1,012 in attendance. On that day the buses brought in 578 people. The church had a staff of four men, all serving full-time and during the year ending had baptized 228 people.

The first staff person in addition to the pastor was Billy Bowen. "Billy has been with us three years," says the pastor. He is only twenty-one years old (1973), but already he is a great gospel singer and one day will be one of the greatest gospel singers in America. The first staff man in our church was a music man because I believe that music plays a vital part in worship and in all the work of the church. It must be good music. It must share the gospel message. It must be music to reach the hearts of the people."

The second staff member is Tom Carrier. Both Carrier and his wife were saved and baptized into the church fellowship in 1971.

He accepted a place on the church staff two years later, being twenty-nine of age at the time. His pastor describes him in glowing terms. "Tom runs about ten feet off the ground," Mosely says. "I mean, Tom runs. I would put him up against anyone in America in personal soul-winning and in creating excitement among bus workers. It's just a real thrill to attend the church bus meeting on Saturday morning and watch him motivate and create excitement among our people. He already is one of the best men I know in the field of evangelism and outreach and is growing all the time."

The third staff member is Jim Gordon. As is true of the Carriers, both Gordon and his wife were saved and baptized in the College Heights church. Gordon was the operator of a large greenhouse business with sales totaling hundreds of thousands of dollars annually. At a tremendous financial sacrifice he assumed a place of service on the College Heights staff. His pastor speaks of him in the same superlatives he uses of the other workers. "He has tremendous organizational ability and an unusually fine soul-winner," he says.

Is it not unusual for a church to select its staff from its own family? Mosely believes this to be a right way to build a church staff. He justifies it for two reasons. "They know what to expect when they begin to work. If I bring in an outsider, he may not know how we do things and he may not fit into our program. These men know me and know how I work. They have lived their lives before us all. They know how to work, and I know how they work. The second reason for getting them out of the church family is that they'll stay with us. These men will stay with me for a lifetime and we can build a solid foundation and then build on it. You cannot have a super-aggressive church without a super-aggressive staff out in front.

In this statement Mosely reveals much of his philosophy and at the same time much of the reason why College Heights has grown. He believes in a super-aggressive church. Halfway measures and halfway effort does not satisfy him personally. He is committed wholly to the task. Nor does he believe such measures and efforts should satisfy a church. The church should take its commitment seriously and bend all possible effort to reach more people for Christ. When asked the reasons for the growth of the church, as he often is asked, his answers grow out of and reflect these convictions. Let him give his own answers to the question.

"The Holy Spirit is sovereign. He cannot be manipulated or maneuvered. We just happened to be in the place where God chose to do a great work and for that we are grateful. We do give God the credit. To boast ourselves would be ridiculous.

"The Pastor Sets the Pattern in Soul-Winning"

"The pastor sets the pattern in soul-winning. Our church staff blocks out all day Tuesday, Tuesday night, and Thursday night for nothing but soul-winning. I will not allow the staff to use this time for anything except soul-winning. Our staff comes out on Tuesday evening and the four of us go soul-winning together.

"We visit almost altogether by appointment. We sit down on Mondays and make appointments over the phone beginning with the 9:00 P.M. appointments first. We make an appointment for 9:00 P.M. Tuesday night, 9:00 P.M. Wednesday night, and 9:00 P.M. Thursday night. We know that we can ordinarily make visits at 7:00 or 7:30, but it's these later hours that are more difficult to make the appointments. So we make them first. If the people will make appointments, this means they're interested. If they're not willing to make appointments, then we usually take this as an indication that they are not interested and our time is not wasted.

"When you launch out into a super-aggressive soul-winning program, you can expect two criticisms: (1) from the negelected members who feel like you're not spending enough time with them, and (2) from the pessimists who say 'What about all of those that we're not holding?' Well, I have discovered that on a percentage basis, we hold as many as a smaller church or a church not growing as fast. Some of these we lose have not really been saved. We can spend hours with these unsaved people and still not hold them. I believe in the security of the believer. When God saves a man, God holds onto him."

"We Emphasize Equipping the Saints"

"We emphasize equipping the saints, taking our cue from Ephesians 4:11-2: 'And he gave some, apostles; and some, prophets; and some, evangelists; and some, pastors and teachers; for the perfecting of the saints, for the work of the ministry, for the edifying of the body of Christ.' This verse is saying four things: (1) God calls leaders, (2) to equip Christians, (3) to minister, and (4) to build the church. The average church today has left out the second part which says to equip Christians. They assume that it is the pastor's responsibility to minister to build the church. This is just simply not God's way. When our church was running around two hundred in Sunday School, I was the evangelistic arm of the church. I did most all the soul-winning. I began to realize that if I were really going to be the pastor to the people and not just their preacher on Sunday morning, then I was going to have to spend more time with them. This meant that my evangelistic arm was cut off. I began to realize that I faced the absolute necessity of equipping my people to minister to be soul-winners if I expected the church to continue to grow."

"We Stress Quality Leadership"

"We stress quality leadership, believing a church must have this to grow. We have preached for years that God will bless a holy people, a pure people. But yet, I'm afraid that we haven't really put it into practice. I believe that one of the greatest reasons that God has blessed College Heights Baptist Church is because of our emphasis upon purity and holiness. All of our deacons and their wives tithe. All of our deacons and wives are soul-winners. They're actively involved in the soul-winning program of the church. The deacons and their wives are above reproach. They cannot serve as deacons if they or their wives smoke or if their personal lives and habits are not above reproach. No deacon is ordained unless he and his wife are involved in all the services of the church. We have a teachers' covenant.

TEACHERS' COVENANT
College Heights Baptist Church

Realizing the importance, privilege and responsibility of teaching in the College Heights Baptist Church Sunday School, I hereby declare:

1. That I will regularly attend and urge members of my class to be present at Sunday morning and evening services, realizing that the Sunday School and the church are inseparable. Unless unavoidably detained, I will regularly attend the midweek prayer service and weekly teachers and officers' meetings (Heb. 10:24-25).
2. That I will be faithful in attendance, arriving at least fifteen minutes early to welcome each pupil as he arrives. If at any time through some unavoidable circumstance I am unable to be present, I will notify my department superintendent as far in advance as possible (1 Cor. 4:2).
3. That I will carefully prepare my lessons and make each class session a matter of earnest prayer. My highest aim as a teacher will be to help my class members to know Christ and accept him as their personal Savior.
4. That I will visit prospects and visitors and be responsible for the absentees in my class, calling upon them in person if possible, or getting in touch with them in some other way to learn the reason for their absence.
5. That I will teach from the open Bible, using the lesson provided by the Sunday School.
6. That I will abstain from the use of intoxicating liquors and tobacco in any form (1 Cor. 6:19).
7. That I will practice the Bible method of tithes and offerings through my class and will teach my class to do likewise. (Gen. 28:22; Mal. 3:8-11; Rom. 2).

This is not just a piece of paper — it is enforced!

"We Have Good Music"

"We have good music. Billy Bowen sings gospel music, music that reaches the hearts and stirs the souls of people. While this is seen as primarily related to the church worship services, it is of great importance in the Sunday School also. Inevitably, the spirit of the church as a whole shapes the Sunday School program."

"We Have Tremendous Excitement"

"There is a tremendous excitement all over our church about winning the lost. We emphasize that the Sunday School is more than an educational arm of the church: it reaches out to find the unsaved, it brings them under the influence of Bible teaching, it creates conditions for people to be saved, it assigns every known evangelistic prospect to someone as his responsibility, it sends a corps of trained soul-winners out, it emphasizes the plan of salvation as a constant theme in teaching, it offers opportunity in the class and department setting for men and women, boys and girls, to make profession of their faith in Jesus as Savior and Lord.

"Excitement in our church includes everything we're doing as a church. Each victory we win increases the joy of the people and leads them to expect something even greater as we follow the Lord and reach out for his blessing."

"Our Church and Our People Think Big"

"Our church and our people think big. Little thinking and expectation of small things is banned. Now, I have discovered the most important person to convince to think big is the pastor. For years I never thought big. But when I finally got over this hurdle myself, I realized that God wanted to do something great in Elyria. I began to look around and saw what God was doing in various churches. I began to believe he wanted to do it here for us. But we must believe that he will.

"The pastor oversees the finances." Now, I know the church controls the finances. But I have discovered that the committee that controls the finances generally controls the church. You can't even start a mission unless this group is behind you and so I began more and more to try to oversee the finances of our church.

"Plan on Staying"

"One of the most detrimental things in Southern Baptist church life is the short-term ministry. Let's not run from our problems.

Baptismal services are frequent at the College Heights Baptist Church of Elyria, Ohio.

In the dead of winter members of College Heights Church view the scene of future church life — the site of new facilities.

Let's not just create problems and leave, let's stay with them and lead our people to be what God expects."

"Key in on Soul-winning Visitation"

"We key in on soul-winning visitation. We have a soul-winning program at 9:15 A.M. Tuesday mornings and 1:00 P.M. on Tuesday afternoon. Our staff goes out Tuesday night. On Thursday night at 7:00 P.M. our church goes out soul-winning and again on Saturday morning at 9:30. I've discovered that if you have one hour for soul-winning, everybody can't show up at that one hour. Why not make it available for them at different hours and let them pick out the most convenient hour? Plus the fact you'll have some of the same people that will come to one, or two, or possibly three sessions of soul-winning. Let me say this about the bus ministry and soul-winning. Church bus evangelism and soul-winning must go hand-in-hand. Just a strong bus ministry will not produce sound solid growth unless you have a strong soul-winning ministry to follow it up and to win the parents of these children. They complement each other. In our soul-winning ministry we stress working with men. I key in on soul-winning with men. This is one of the reasons we do go soul-winning by appointment. We can catch the men at home."

"Use Bus Ministry"

"We use the bus ministry. We began two bus ministries and both times we failed. The first time we just bought one white bus and it never got off the ground! Someone came along and said, "You've got to have more than one bus." We bought five. We still failed! Bill Powell, who was with the Home Mission Board at that time, came and shared with us insights on how to really utilize church bus evangelism. And since that day, church bus evangelism has been our greatest tool.

"Following a recent bus conference we added 6 new buses and 5 new routes. We had our record high of 1,012 in Sunday School. On that day, we ran 12 bus routes with 4 new "baby" routes and had 578 people ride our buses. One captain, Frank Mollard, had 136 people ride one bus. Since that time we've given Frank another bus. To reach that 136, Frank visited 20 hours on his route.

Our Sunday School teachers, to better appreciate and understand the bus ministry, are required to visit at least 4 hours on our bus routes. God has used this to open our teachers eyes. We have graded worship services for our children. We have two Beginner worship services, one for four-year-olds and one for five-year-olds. We have a Primary worship service of first, second, and third grades, and a Junior worship of fourth, fifth, and sixth grades. I believe that church bus evangelism is the greatest single tool for evangelism that I have ever seen in my life. It will open more doors and provide more soul-winning opportunities than any other method. It's the best way to discover prospects. It is an unbelievable tool that every church willing to pay the price of hard work ought to have. We believe that the day will come when we will have one hundred buses running in this area.

For church bus evangelism to be successful, the church staff must set the pattern. If there is just one man on the staff, he ought to be the church bus director and be the captain of one of those buses. He's saying to his people, 'Here's how to do it and I'll show you the way.' I would not have a man on my staff that would not first be a bus captain and have fifty on a route at least four times. How could a staff man rejoice? How could a minister of education rejoice when a bus captain had fifty on his bus unless he had really experienced the joy himself? How could he possibly know about the hard work involved? It's hard work but it pays tremendous dividends."

"Give to World Missions"

"Let me point out one mistake that I made. Notice that I did not say that I just made one mistake — I'm just pointing out one. For about six or seven months I let our church slip by and give only token gifts to World Missions through the Cooperative Program. This was a grievous sin and a terrible mistake on my part. It is not either . . . or. We must be both in our Jerusalem and in the uttermost part of the earth at the same time."

Presently College Heights church works within and without a $260,000 facility with 12,000 square feet of space. Directly across the street is a 250-acre, 12 million dollar college campus. Next door is an elementary school. To care for the people who crowd in on

Sundays the church rents space from both the college across the street and the elementary school which touches its own property. The auditorium seats 500 people; it is crowded on Sunday morning as the pastor preaches to the saved. The auditorium is nearly filled on Sunday evenings when the pastor leads an evangelistic service and preaches to the unsaved, quite different from the usual church. People are everywhere about this church, not bulging at the seams, but with the seams long since burst asunder. What will the church do?

As Mosely said, the church is thinking big. It is purchasing twenty-three acres of land at a major interstate system cloverleaf connection. This new property is between two cities, Lorain and Elyria. When completed, Interstate 90 will make the city of Cleveland within twenty-five minutes of the new location. Will the church take advantage of that fact. Yes. They expect to see the day they'll have a hundred buses, some running right into Cleveland itself. They expect to see the Sunday School reach five thousand.

"The story of College Heights is not the story of one man," Mosely cautions. "It is the story of many people. Their dedication and commitment to Christ continue to amaze me. If the Lord tarries in his coming, their dreams and visions, the dreams and visions of our church, will be accomplished."

The Ridgeland Baptist Church of Ridgeland, Mississippi, located near Jackson,

6

Finding Excitement in Reaching People

Ridgeland Baptist Church
Ridgeland, Mississippi

Ridgeland Baptist Church is located in a community of three thousand people ten miles north of Jackson, Mississippi. In 1970 the Sunday School attendance average stood at 184, a decline of ten over the previous two years. The attendance essentially was static, for the following two years saw it remain at 187.

Then the Sunday School began to grow. By 1973 the attendance level had risen to four hundred. This gain of 113 would be impressive for a large church, but for a small church it is especially significant. During the two-year period several "big days" had seen attendance figures for the one Sunday go above nine hundred and once above one thousand.

The catalyst of growth, at least in part, was the dedicated commitment of Jerry Odom, who came to the church as pastor in July, 1971. Odom is a native of Mississippi and a graduate of Mississippi College. He is also a graduate of Southwestern Baptist Theological Seminary with the degree Master of Religious Education. Before coming to Ridgeland he had served as pastor of Hillcrest Baptist Church, Suffolk, Virginia, and as associate pastor of the Southside Baptist Church of Meridian Mississippi. About the time he came to Ridgeland as pastor, he says he became convinced that a committed pastor leading a committed church can achieve anything the church wants to do for the glory of Christ. With that kind of commitment he challenged the church to move ahead. According to Odom, the following sequence of events tells the story of the growth of the church.

October, 1971. Four months after the new pastor arrived, a rally day was set for the purpose of setting a new Sunday School attendance record. The old record was 265. On rally day the three hundred barrier was broken for the first time as 350 attended. This experience was only the beginning of many records to be set and broken in the next year. The Sunday School enrollment was only 362!

March, 1972. Five months later the Sunday School was averaging 237 in attendance. The pastor challenged the Sunday School to average 301 for the next six weeks. An attendance campaign was mounted and during this campaign the Sunday School went over the three hundred mark three times, setting a new record at 358 and averaging 306 for the six weeks. Enrollment reached 423.

April, 1972. A lay evangelism school was conducted to train Adults and Youth how to share their faith. Eighty enrolled and attended the five nights of training which included on-the-job training. Six months later another school was conducted, and the church visitation-witnessing program has from 20 to 25 adults who go every week to witness to the lost. A continuing witness-training program trains more witnesses. The church baptized 108 persons and received by transfer 80 persons in 1972.

May, 1972. A bus outreach program was begun. For two years the pastor had been reading, studying, and praying about the bus ministry and was convinced of its value. In January of 1972 he challenged the church to enter the bus ministry. After months of preparation, the church began with two buses and brought in 20 riders the first week. On the first Sunday one of the riders, a little girl, accepted Christ as Savior.

In the sixth week, riders numbered 71. On the tenth week a third bus was added. On the twelfth week attendance reached 162 on three buses. During the seventeenth week a fourth bus was added and on the twenty-third week 200 riders came in on the buses.

The church purchased three more buses for a total of seven buses. On January 28, the buses brought in 301 riders.

God has used these buses and their workers and riders to inject a spirit of conquest never before experienced. Many have been saved and baptized. Three graded worship services are conducted each week for more than 100 boys and girls, ages four to eleven. The involvement of the church in this outreach program stimulated all aspects of the church, such as missions, training, and finances. All reached new heights and records.

June, 1972. During the last week in May the pastor challenged the Sunday School again to new heights. The word "slump" was banned, never again to be used in reference to the summer. Instead the Summer Sunday School SURGE was begun. The goal was to average 271 for the three summer months. This was 21 above the average to date (Oct.-May, 250).

The results:

	Average Attendance	
	1971	1972
June	173	300
July	169	360
August	178	369
Averages	173	343

An average of 170 more in Sunday School each week than the previous year and 72 more than the goal set.

July, 1972. During a revival which emphasized personal soul-winning and bus outreach as well as evangelistic services, attendance broke all revival meeting records. Prior to this week the church had baptized forty and received fifty-five by transfer of letter. During the revival there were seventy-one professions of faith, sixteen transfers of membership, and scores of rededication.

October, 1972. At the close of the revival in July, the late evangelist Ray Sadler challenged the pastor and church to have a "miracle day" in October. The object of the "miracle day" was to set a goal for Sunday School attendance that the church thought it could achieve plus 100, which by faith the Lord would add and thus a miracle would be performed. A goal of 800 was set; more than double the 350 a year ago. An aggressive plan of promotion was followed. Sunday School class goals were set. Individuals were asked to sign a commitment card to attend. Invitations to out-of-town friends were mailed. The day finally arrived and so did the people. A total of 903 registered their attendance in a church which had at the time 500 church members and 660 enrolled in Sunday School. Praise God for the miracle.

January, 1973. The first annual January Bible conference was held January 28-31, 1973. The conference was kicked off by Super Sunday, when 950 attended Sunday School. The conference averaged 425, which was the average Sunday School attendance.

April, 1973. The Sunday School broke the one thousand barrier. A giant rally day, called Super Sunday, was staged. Paul Anderson, "the world's strongest man," was scheduled as a speaker and the program was geared toward attracting large numbers of youth. "This young man has a good testimony and he preaches the gospel just as a pastor would," said Odom. On this Sunday the Sunday School reached an attendance of 1,026.

In July, 1973, at the invitation of A. V. Washburn, secretary of the Sunday School Department of the Sunday School Board, Odom spoke at one of the Sunday School weeks at the Glorieta Baptist Conference Center. Requested to tell of the work of Ridgeland Sunday School, he described it in terms of a Christian task force.

Bus Outreach Is the Marine Corps.

"We look upon our bus evangelism program as the Marine Corps of our church," he said. "In pursuing an objective the Marines hit the beaches first. Our bus program does that; its workers are responsible for making the first visits into the homes of those whom we hope to reach. Bright and early every Saturday morning they are at the church. After a breakfast and some time for inspiration and prayer, out they go into the community. They work four hours, six hours, all day long, and when the day is ended they have the names of those who will ride the buses the following morning and also fresh new prospects to add to the list of our specific responsibilities. Literally, they cover the community and they discover and have discovered hundreds of prospects."

"Here is one thing God is using in this day that gives immediate results," continued Odom. "As an educational director, an associate pastor, and as a pastor I tried to reach people using the tools and methods I knew but I never seemed to get quick results. A bus program changed that. The people go out all day Saturday visiting and the next morning they see results of their labor. Those results usually are exciting. People like to be involved in things that are moving and are showing results.

The Sunday School Is the Army.

"The joy of the army is to go in, seize the territory, and hold it," the pastor continued. "This is exactly what the Sunday School forces do. The Sunday School is the largest organization of the church, but beyond that it has the organizational structure to assign the responsibility for ministering to every individual prospect to a specific class and even to a specific person in the class. Someone responsible for every prospect and someone responsible for the spiritual growth and development of every church member — this is the beauty of the Sunday School organization.

"We use the Sunday School for evangelism. Our goal is that every Sunday in the older Children's departments, the Youth, and the Adult classes, the plan of salvation will be presented in an understandable way and that the teacher will make a continuing effort to enroll unsaved persons and then to win them to Jesus.

Odom assigned the weekly teachers and officers' meeting a key place in his Sunday School evangelism emphasis. "Just as an army could not go into the field against an enemy without adequate training, so a Sunday School cannot function as an army for evangelism without continuing training," he said. "An army must know how to do its job." The officers and teachers' meeting, he pointed out, affords workers an opportunity to evaluate their work the previous week, to inspire each other for the work, and to prepare for the coming Sunday's effort. He mentioned further the need for improving teaching methods and pointed to the weekly meeting as the best vehicle for achieving this objective.

The Ridgeland Sunday School is goal-oriented. It sets quarterly goals for enrollment and attendance, setting these goals to emphasize the gains expected and to be worked for. Once each year it engages in an attendance campaign for a period of six weeks. It may engage in an enrollment campaign from time to time. Several times each year it promotes a peak attendance thrust.

The Lay Evangelism Group Are the Special Forces.

"The bus evangelism group discovers the prospects. The Sunday School workers follow up. The lay evangelism group goes out to witness."

These workers were trained in the lay evangelism schools conducted by the church. These schools, using the program developed and suggested by the Evangelism Division of the Home Mission Board and the WIN materials, produced a corps of some twenty-five or thirty trained witnesses. Some, but not all, are adults; the youth are well represented and make effective witnesses. "We followed the plans word for word," Odom said. "We cut no corners, we carried out every detail. We continued with the witness training activities following each of the schools we conducted." The result? A group goes out every week to witness — and folks are being saved week by week.

Those trained in the lay evangelism program, trained in witnessing and counseling, are used on Sundays as counselors. Every person who responds to an invitation, regardless of his reason or the nature of his decision, is assigned a personal counselor. In a counseling room the counselor offers guidance and help. Those who make professions of faith receive four follow-up visits in their homes.

We Use the Big Day Philosophy.

Here Odom failed to carry through with his comparison of the church and Sunday School to an army for Christ. He might have said that the big day gave his forces an opportunity for regrouping and facing the next objective. This is the way he seemed to be using the big day.

"Once a year we do something so spectacular in our church and through our church that it will gain the attention of the non-church going public of our community," Odom said. "That is, we pull out all the stops and we have a really big day. The church may bring in an outside feature for the big day or it may use the pastor as the main speaker, but regardless of what is done, tremendous enthusiasm is generated." What does a big day do for the church? Odom points out that on one of these days the Sunday School gained sixty or seventy-five new prospects who could be followed up.

"Now then this is what we are doing. Bus outreach, good Sunday School work, lay evangelism, and the extra special something to attract the attention of the public," he summarized. "Our church is out of the way between an old highway and a super highway. It's cut off literally from where people live. We have no signs or billboards, but people know about our church. They know what we preach and what we stand for. It's because we try to be faithful to the Word of God, exercising our faith and working hard to the greater glory of our Lord."

In August 1973, Odom received a call from the First Baptist

Church of Galena Park, Texas, in the Houston metropolitan area. He moved to Galena Park. The immediate question became: What will happen to the church now that the dynamic pastor has gone? Will it lose its gain? Will the excitement disappear? Will attendance drop to the former level? Or will the church continue to advance? Will it make still further gains?

This question is always answered when a pastor leaves a church for a new work. It became especially pertinent in the case of "The Exciting Ridgeland Baptist Church," and especially pertinent for this book on fastest growing Sunday Schools. Can a church, led to initiate an aggressive program, continue through an interim and into a succeeding pastorate?

A part of the answer comes from Robert McDonald, associate pastor, on whom the responsibility for the church fell during the interim. During this period he assessed the situation.

"Naturally we felt a great loss. For two years Brother Odom had been a powerful figure and a fine leader in our church. I had recently come as associate pastor and didn't know the program real well, but the people pledged support and asked me to do my best.

"The church went through a transitional period. Both the new Christians and the old church members felt a closeness to the man who had been their pastor. However, through the program he promoted and through his personal attitude and witness he had led them to a closer walk with the Lord Jesus.

"Our Sunday School attendance continues above 400. On the first Sunday of October (1973) we had 472 and our average for this month (October) is 435. On the last Sunday of the month we promoted a high attendance day and reached 600 in attendance. The witness training and the witnessing activities continue and the bus workers labor as effectively as ever. Every Sunday someone is saved in our services."

At Walnut Street Baptist Church there is a full program of educational and worship experiences . . .

. . . but the congregation realizes that it must continually move out into the community. Here bus workers and riders are inspired.

7

Using the Inner City as an Opportunity in Reaching People

Walnut Street Baptist Church
Louisville, Kentucky

The Walnut Street Baptist Church is located in the heart of Louisville, Kentucky's inner city. What does being located in the inner city mean to a church? Usually, death or relocation.

The Situation of the Inner-City Church

To see how true this is, begin at the Walnut Street Church and move three or four blocks in any direction. The great downtown churches of yesteryear are gone. Where they stood are now new office buildings of just vacant lots.

Broadway Baptist Church once rivaled Walnut Street as to which would have the largest Sunday School frequently having more in attendance and was the largest in the state in the forties and fifties. It has gone to the suburbs. The Downtown Presbyterian Church is gone, the property cleared off. The great church of the Methodist Conference, one block from Walnut Street at the corner of Fourth and St. Katherine, has a great old gothic building like Walnut Street but only a weak congregation. Their leading churches now are St. Paul's out in the suburbs and Christ Methodist Church also there. The downtown Episcopal Cathedral, Christ Church, struggles to stay alive while surburban Episcopal churches thrive in their new areas, new property, and new buildings.

One block from Walnut Street church is another congregation that just collapsed and folded up. The building is still there, a church building walled up and used for other purposes. Three blocks further up the street stands another abandoned church building. At least fifteen empty buildings or vacant lots can be seen within a mile, where churches have gone, disappeared, or moved to the suburbs. There are eight or ten other churches in the larger area near that are just struggling to stay alive with a few people in great massive buildings built for great congregations of yesterday.

This condition results from the change in the city itself. This, too, can be seen by walking from Walnut Street, a few blocks in any direction. The church stands at the edge of the business district. Start two blocks away and move north toward the Ohio river; you find business solid. Start in the other direction, however, and you have walked through a belt of the old houses, the old mansions of yesterday still with the carriage houses in the backyards, or, better, great courtyards behind the houses. Drive down the alleys and you see the carriage houses, the courtyards, and the massive brick and stone buildings that once were mansions. Now they are old, deteriorating apartment houses, cut up into eight-ten-fifteen kitchenette apartments.

This is the first stop for the white Appalachian who comes to the city, uneducated and unemployed. Yet the area is racially mixed, about half black and half white. The poorest of the black and the poorest of the whites are mixed together, and they're solid packed and jammed all around the church. Here, of course is found one of the highest crime rates in the city. The church has alcoholism and drug addiction right at its doorstep all the time. The houses of prostitution are near, one of the largest and most notorious ones in Louisville said to be only three blocks from the church. There's mugging, purse snatching, and all kinds of petty crime.

Now what has happened to the church? Well the church — great massive gothic architecture that could hardly be reproduced today as it would be so expensive, is a beautiful church. But it has an aging membership. It has a membership that has been static and stagnant for a long time. The church membership in 1940 was 3,849 people. Church membership in 1950 was 5,058. Church membership in 1960 was 4,895 people.

Wayne Dehoney came to the church as pastor on February 1, 1967. He had become acquainted with the church when he was a student at Southern Baptist Theological Seminary. Since then the church has changed, of course. Dehoney had accumulated years of experience in church development as pastor of Central Park Baptist Church in Birmingham, Alabama, and at First Baptist Church in Jackson, Tennessee.

"The church had come face-to-face with the fact that it was slipping," Dehoney says in talking about his first days with the people. "It had 4,761 people, but I found that it was an aged member-ship. The young adults had moved to the surburbs, the church had not perpetuated itself, there was a poverty of young adults and a shortage of children. What children they were reaching were largely neighborhood children. It was a graying congregation, but it still was a church with some great assets.

"First of all it had fine facilities. It had some capable and dedi-cated leadership among the older people. Perhaps its greatest asset was its basic commitment to evangelism. The people believed in reaching people. They believed in evangelism at its best. They called themselves an evangelistic church.

"It considered itself a people's church — not a socially elite church. It did not feel that it was better or superior. It was also a church with a genuine concern for people. Talk about people's needs, about suffering, about lostness, and the people responded deeply, emotion-ally, and financially.

"So the church wanted to reach people, it wanted to be evangelis-tic, it wanted to grow. It had this kind of commitment.

"In addition to these great assets the church also had a spirit of commitment to conservative biblical theology. The membership con-sidered themselves a conservative church in a conservative state. They did not seek the liberal road in any way. They believed the Bible to be the basis for faith and practice, they wanted the Bible preached, they wanted it taught, and they wanted it to be the basis of whatever the church did.

"None of us saw the clear way," continues the pastor with a smile. The smile alerts us that even though the way could not be seen then, it was found. God revealed the way and led the church into it for the church is filled with people of all ages and from all walks of life. Attendance in Sunday School has risen to 1,466 from 950 in 1970. This is a gain of 516 in the three years, again to justify saying the great old church has a fast growing Sunday School. Numbers never tell all the story; always it is bigger than the measurement ap-plied to it. How has the spiritual and numerical growth been achieved? Begin at the church door and work out.

"We said we're going to reach the people at our doorstep." De-honey states. "We're not going to jump over them and simply have a cathedral church downtown to which suburbanites come. We're going to make an honest and sincere, fervent, and zealous effort to reach the people at our doorstep.

Now as a result, 25 percent of the church membership comes from the immediate community round about. These people are being reached. They're difficult to reach, difficult to hold, difficult to integrate or mix with the older and more established membership. Yet the church has succeeded in doing the difficult. There are both blacks and whites; the church overcame the racial barrier. More than one hundred blacks attend Sunday School. They sing in the church choir and the youth choirs. Balck adults have come on transfer of membership to join with Walnut Street. Further, the church has both social and economic levels. Dehoney preaches on Sunday to Ph.D's from the University of Louisville and professors from the seminary and also to adults who are functional illiterates, who neither can read or write. The broad span of all humanity is there.

The church recognized it must do more than reach those nearby. It was compelled to gear its programs to reach into the outlying areas and pull the suburbanite downtown.

The problem is that the inner city cannot sustain its own institutions, and the immediate community about Walnut Street cannot provide for itself, the church, and the church program it needs. It has neither the financial resources nor the leadership ability to do it. The resources are out in the suburbs and the needs are in the inner city. So the problem of the church effectively is to match and mix the needs of the inner city with the resources of the suburbs. The suburbs have the resources of leadership and the resources of finance, but the church must get people down the expressways, past a half-dozen other churches, committed and ready to give their leadership ability and their money and to mix their families and their children in with the needs of the inner city and all its problems.

Reaching the suburbs means a two-pronged church program, a program to reach the most elite, sophisticated, educated suburbanite and at the same time reach the most underprivileged person, deprived socially, economically, and in every other way. Yet the church is not divided into two units. It does not have two kinds of Sunday Schools — that is, a neighborhood Sunday School and a suburbanite Sunday School. People are together in the same Sunday School classes.

Make Evangelism the Spearhead

Another commitment the church made was that everything done would be to the end of evangelism. Evangelism is the spearhead; everything must serve this ultimate end. If an action of a church project does not serve this end of evangelism the church believes it has no business doing it. Evangelism is the priority and the many multiple programs are developed as means to this end. For example, the church extensive recreation program and a wide-ranging social ministry are two such programs. These are important in themselves, but they are important also because they open doors of evangelistic opportunity.

"Just to minister, just to say we give food because people are hungry, is not enough," says the pastor. "If we do not purpose to minister to the larger hunger, the spiritual hunger, if you satisfy only the physical need, we think that we've missed the mark as a church. So our commitment is that everything we do is to the end of evangelism."

Minister to the Whole Man

Dehoney enlarged upon his statements concerning evangelism by saying that church endeavors to minister to the whole man. "We use the word 'whole,'" he says.

"We talk about the whole gospel and ministering to the whole man. This means that we are concerned about a person's whole nature. We endeavor to minister to the person physically, we minister to him socially, and we minister to him spiritually. If we simply reach a woman in the neighborhood through a Sunday School class and win her to Christ, then tell her we are not concerned about her housing needs, not concerned about the fact that she has three boys and all three of them are behind in their school work and about to drop out and have no motivation, and if we do not care that she comes wringing her hands and saying she doesn't know what to do, they're on the streets and they're getting involved in petty crime, then we're not preaching the whole gospel. Nor are we applying the whole gospel.

"So we used this word 'whole.' It means the whole man, the whole gospel, the whole family, the whole community, the whole of humanity. This means black and white, whoever comes when we

Walnut Street occasionally leaves the baptistry to baptize in a nearby river.

Walnut Street has a ministry to all ages and interests, as evidenced by this sewing class for "golden agers."

preach the gospel or whoever we see when we go out visiting. This meant the hippy in our community and we went through an era when we were reaching lots of hippies. We need to be concerned about the need of the drug addict among this group. And so we've used this word 'whole.' I think it's a marvelous summary statement, of the gospel.

Involve People in Planning and Reaching

How does a leader come to grips with a church that has lost its young adults, is losing in membership, and has a Sunday School declining steadily? Dehoney's answer and the answer of Walnut Street was participation by the entire membership. Many committees were appointed and studies were made of the needs of the church. They determined what long-range goals should be. One of the most exciting things done was involving the church membership in brainstorming sessions. People wrote out everything that they thought their church might do, no matter how "wild" it might seem. They got more than two hundred suggestions fed in. Out of these the survey committee selected and organized concepts and came up with basic fundamental programs. They became the church priorities and goals.

Pulpit-centered Ministry

The pulpit and the preaching of the gospel is the center of the ministry of the church. The importance of the pulpit is made plain. The pulpit must be evangelistic, it must be stimulating. The people insist the pulpit be effective. It must be biblical, conservative, and relevant to life.

The centrality of the pulpit ministry is emphasized through a color telecast of the services. Dehoney believes this to be one of the most productive things the church does. The televising of the Sunday morning service has become a means whereby outreach of the church to the community is felt. It secures the attention of the city as a whole and brings people out of the suburbs into the city. "I frequently preach on the program of our church and our commitment. I simply say to all the city that Walnut Street is your church down in the heart of your city doing what we believe the church ought to do and we invite listeners to come down to a live, dynamic, growing church. I speak of our church as one vitally relevant to the needs of men and yet bases its faith in the Bible," Dehoney says.

Place Sunday School in Lead

"Give priority to the Sunday School as the main-line educational program of the church," Dehoney says. "It takes the lead." Now we faced a problem in that we had a dual Sunday School, in that we had a graded Sunday School along beside an ungraded Sunday School. Attempts had been made ten years before to grade the Sunday School but it had failed miserably, a great conflict, lots of bitterness, lots of hostility over this.

"Actually, that effort was made way back in 1956. I guess it was when they went into the new building and another effort was made after that. Convention-wide workers were brought in and the old traditional element in the church resisted, the big Bible classes resisted, and as a result they wound up with one graded structure as one Sunday School and this whole bunch of ungraded Adult classes. There were far more enrolled in the ungraded segment of the Adult Division than there were in the graded segment of Adults which was very weak. But we said we're going to commit ourselves to reaching people through the Sunday School and we're not going to get hung up on methods.

"I agreed that we weren't going to fight the issue of grading. I feel like we could function a lot better if we were graded from top to bottom, but we're going to love these ungraded classes. We're just going to consider them a part of everything we did and yet we said we're going to build and keep and maintain a strong graded structure and try to feed prospects — new people — into the graded structure and in time solve our problem. This is really what's happening today as the ungraded classes get older and older and the live dynamic units which are growing are the graded units and here's where we start our new units and produce our new growth.

"So I decided we would not have a battle over this and that the spirit of outreach was more important, the fellowship and cooperation was more important, and we geared ourselves to reach people through all of these units."

Develop Social Ministries

The church has organized broad, comprehensive, and innovative social ministries programs. All around great social needs were evident: hunger, poverty, joblessness, domestic problems of all kinds. The first staff member Dehoney added was a trained social worker, a person trained in the ministry and church work but also professionally trained as a social worker. Out of this social ministries emphasis came a number of individual programs. Among them were a work and a clothing shop.

Each week the church gives hundred of articles of clothing and bedding material to people. This is clothing the people bring in; it's repaired by the Fellowship Club — a group of women for this purpose who meet each Thursday. They sew and repair the clothing or they make it into quilts. For this work they have a battery of sewing machines — about twenty. The Fellowship repairs the clothing, cleans it, and hangs it for distribution as gifts or through the church thrift shop or clothing shop. The church also has a food closet. The people bring food in. It is stocked at church and given to fill needs.

For a time the church operated a health office in a store front building a block from the church. Manned by volunteers from the church, it cost little money because most of the people's needs could be met by social agencies already in existence. Yet it rendered a significant help because so many did not know where to get help — legal assistance, medicine. This was an effort in the name of Christ to give a cup of cold water.

The church also has sponsored a tutoring program. This effective program matched on a one-to-one basis or one-to-two basis suburban young people, high school students, school teachers and retired people, with youth both in and out of the membership, but needing help. A young person who has lost motivation and is about to drop out of school needs help. The church found a way to supply the greatest need, motivation.

Among other things in the social ministries program, the church operates a mental health clinic four days a week in the church. This began in cooperation with the state mental health program.

Another is a drug rehabilitation house or center operated by a woman who is called affectionately Earth Mother. The house is a live-in situation for both boys and girls. It is rigidly controlled but is a complete Christian answer to drug addiction. This All-the-Way

House is across the street from the church and is a part of its total program. The courts refer young people to the director and probate them to her if she agrees to take them into All-the-Way House. She has high return on drug cures; the solution is entirely Christian involving putting Christ in the center of the person's life and living under the rigid disciplines of Bible study and all-out commitment to Christ twenty-four hours a day.

The Neighborhood Development Corporation was a cooperative venture on the part of several churches of the area, a nonprofit corporation dedicated to taking this immediate area, Old Louisville, and turning it around, getting it restored with people moving back. The idea is to stop the decay, both property and economic decay. Walnut Street placed $2,500 into a budget the first year, other churches also supported it. The newspaper became interested and sent an urban reporter specialist to learn what was happening. The Catholic college of the area, Katherine Spalding College, along with some businesses became a part. The University of Louisville with their Urban Studies Department became a part and secured a federal grant.

As a result of the work of this group, Old Louisville was turned around and now is coming back up. Old houses are being salvaged and renovated. For professional people to come to the area has become popular. High-rise apartments have been built. The church is happy and proud to have had a part in meeting these needs.

The church itself led the way. It built a high-rise apartment called Baptist Towers directly across and in front of the church, a seventeen-story, 199-unit retirement center. It is full with a waiting list.

Bus Outreach

The bus outreach program of the church is led by lay persons, rather than by a person on the church staff. Nine bus routes operate under the supervision of a dentist, Dr. Carl Kuhl. Dr. Kuhl is a committed deacon who caught a vision. He attended several bus clinics to learn and then initiated the program. He enlists bus pastors, bus drivers, and youth workers. He promotes the work and also conducts the youth church service. There is also a children's worship service and a preschool group that is the extended nursery program.

In summarizing, Dr. Dehoney says he wants to speak to others. "I believe that any church can grow and reach people in any situation," he says. "I don't think I could have said this with authority before I came to Walnut Street because I'd never been faced with exactly the same situation as this. I've been in suburban churches where people are just falling in all around and know the suburban churches can grow. I've been in county seat towns where the First Baptist Church had prestige, where it was the center, where the pulpit had influence, where the pastor was a respected citizen of the community. But I had never been in a downtown, inner-city situation where all of the institutions of the inner city had suffered, the businesses were closed, the schools gone down and the churches folded. I had never faced the real racial problems. We had a riot in Louisville, for example, two years after I came here and there was looting and burning two blocks from our church.

"Now I can say that I've been in about every kind of a situation, and I can say that a church can grow. It can reach people wherever it is, wherever the circumstances are if (1) it has leadership, leadership that is committed to reaching people and leadership that leads, leadership that's willing to pay the price of leadership to get out in front, to set an example and a challenge and show this commitment all the time; and if (2) it will define its goals clearly. Leadership must help the church define its goals in evangelism and its goals in outreach. I think a church can grow if (3) it has a basic fundamental commitment to evangelism. Without this a church will not grow. Many churches are concerned only about ministering to themselves. They're concerned only about in-depth study and training.

"People grow by their involvement in reaching others for Christ, and witnessing to those who need Christ. I think a fourth necessary ingredient to growth is that the church must be biblically oriented. It must have what I call a conservative biblical approach to its ministry, to its pulpit, to its theology, that this is its basis of authority and this is its basis for the message that it communicates. I think, also, if a church is to grow, it must have a certain spirit of flexibility, a willingness to try anything. It must be willing to experiment and to innovate. The church must be willing to try anything and to do anything to reach people."

8

Using Proven Methods in Reaching People

Curtis Baptist Church
Augusta, Georgia

The Curtis Baptist Church is located in downtown Augusta, Georgia, a sleepy southern town with an area population of 175,000. Prior to 1960, for five consecutive years it shared the losses being suffered by many downtown churches. It lost in Sunday School enrollment and attendance. It declined also in number of baptisms, finances, and even in total church membership. The church membership wondered if there could be found a way to reverse the trend.

In 1960 Lawrence V. Bradley, Jr., assumed the pastorate and the leadership of the church. At that time the Sunday School had 1,010 enrolled with an average attendance of 479. By 1973, 4,692 new members had been received into the church and the membership had made a gain of 2,392.

How has the Sunday School fared? As the lead organization of the Curtis Baptist Church, its growth has parallelled and been involved in all the growth the church has achieved. In the thirteen-year period of time the Sunday School has enrolled 7,165 new members, an average of 1.5 persons per day, week after week and year after year. This growth has been a consistent growth across the years. As reported to the church in 1970 average attendance in the Sunday School was 1,023 and three years later, in 1973, rose to 1,389. This is a gain in these three years of 366. In the months of September and October, 1973, the attendance level held at about 1,450. Curtis is continuing to grow in Bible study.

Other areas of church life and activity also continue to grow.

Three major building programs have been completed, including the acquisition of additional property for parking and expansion, and the total church property (a city block) is now valued at $3,322,075.00. One mission was constituted a church at which time 201 members became charter members of the new church. Curtis Church also has a fully accredited Christian day school (founded in

1963), kindergarten through the tenth grade. The eleventh and twelveth grades will be added in the next two years. Present enrollment of 857 with an operating budget of $500,000. Total income for all purposes for the current year is $916,906.25.

How did all this come about? If you listen to the members of Curtis Church they will tell you it is the use of Lawrence Bradley by the Lord. Bradley, however, credits a people "chosen for his name."

"All we've done," he says, "has been because of the commitment and dedication of the people. I have a congregation of people who believe the Bible and follow it. I am fortunate also to have a people who believe in their pastor and follow his leadership."

"I can't praise my laymen enough," he says. "I have found my older members very progressive in a day when we think vision is limited to young men."

Beyond this, what are some of the discernible reasons for the growth of this Sunday School?

A Commitment to Serve the Entire City from a Downtown Location

This is a two-pronged statement for the commitment is in two directions. First, it is a commitment to the downtown location, and second it is a commitment to serve all the city. This states well the attitude of the pastor and the leadership of the church.

"Should the downtown church move out?" Bradley asked his people in his thirteenth anniversary sermon to them. He answered, "Both yes and no. It should not move out geographically, but it should move out in service." He then listed seven problems which he sees facing the downtown church, including Christ.

(1) Parking. Adequate parking is a must.
(2) Pull of other churches. Suburban church contend with downtown churches.
(3) Scattered membership. Members live in all areas of a metro region.
(4) Transportation. This particularly applies to children.
(5) Recreation. This includes week-day activities.
(6) Leadership. Leadership must be trained to be effective.
(7) Visitation. Visitation is necessary to reaching people.
(8) Property. To reach people buildings and space are needed.

At the conclusion of the message the pastor ringingly stated his commitment to the downtown location. "The downtown church is destined to lose some of its members to suburban churches," he said. "But there are others to be reached. We must find them, invite them, and enlist them. The mission of the church is to go. The preacher is to care. The staff is to care. You, the people of the church, are to care. Let the program of Curtis be that of taking Christ to the Christless; God to the godless; grace to the ungraceful; and help to the helpless. Unless we do, we might as well lock the door and throw away the key.

"Should the downtown church move out?" he asked again. "In the expansion of its program, yes. In the maintenance and enlargement of its buildings, yes. In its effort to reach the city for Christ, yes. In its missionary vision, yes."

The challenge was the more effective because it reflected the philosophy Bradley has followed in the thirteen years he has led Curtis, a philosophy his people share with him.

Since a commitment is an attitude, however, its meaning is best seen in the manner through which it expresses itself. What has Curtis done through the years to express its basic commitment to reach people, all the city, from its downtown location?

A Many-faceted Enlargement of the Sunday School Organization

Tried and proven Southern Baptist methods and materials are used, but new and innovative approaches are welcomed and encouraged.

Recognizing that reaching more people requires a larger organization, multiple departments and multiple Bible study units are provided. Constantly the organization is evaluated and places for new teaching units are determined. The church believes it has enough workers available in its membership to staff whatever organization is needed and as the nominating committee works with the educational staff it finds a ready response when people are offered places of service. Training of workers is considered a must and the Wednesday night officers and teachers' meeting is used as the pivot for training.

Beyond this, which Bradley looks upon as "the organization every

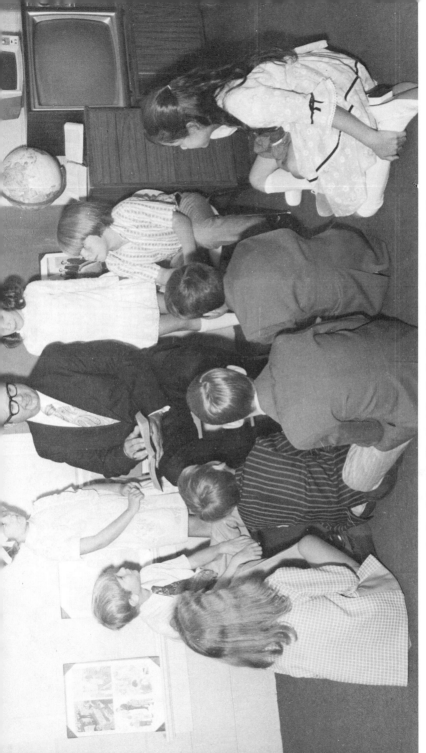

Sunday School is "fun" at the Curtis Baptist Church of Augusta, Ga.

Southern Baptist church knows best," the Sunday School has developed many Bible study opportunities for many special groups.

1. A department for the deaf. — The church has a professionally trained interpreter. This is a strong department that reaches twenty-five people in Bible study each Sunday morning. *Simplified Bible Study,* the Sunday School Board Life and Work quarterly, is used for the curriculum. Sunday evening finds the interpreter training additional hearing people as interpreters.

2. A department for the slow learner. — This department might be called the Special Education department. It is not large, but it meets a definite need. The church sends a key leader of this department to Ridgecrest Conference Center each summer.

3. A department for the blind. — Through the years, denominational leaders in the main have suggested that these be a natural part of a regular Bible study unit. It has been thought unwise to have a special class for them. The experience and study of Curtis indicated, however, that group was not being reached by their existing classes. To meet a need, the minister of education organized a department for the blind. Fortunately, the church had in its membership a woman who could teach Braille. The church does not suggest that every church have a department for this group; Curtis Baptist set this one up to meet a special need.

4. A department for alcoholics. — All churches have people who face this problem, but a downtown church feels it more keenly. Curtis was bombarded constantly by people in need because of this problem. Many want food or clothing, but a large number of alcoholics wandered in off the streets. If such a person is going through withdrawal, or says he feels like killing someone, there is no time to check a "job description." That's the time for ministry. Curtis Church has been able to help in reclaiming many such, who are now members. They help greatly in a ministry of compassion and love. One of these is the teacher of a department for men who are alcoholics. As many as twenty-four have been present in this department. These men need help and they know it.

5. A department for single adults. — Some of these are career single adults, but many are divorced. Feeling that churches too long have stood back condemned, Curtis tries to do something in a concrete way to minister to these people. Some are victims of circumstances, but whatever the circumstances, the church feels a need to provide for them and help them spiritually. Curtis has a department for unmarried adults that goes through age thirty-five. Two classes are active — one for ladies and one for men.

In Matthew 25:31-46 Christ spoke of people who were in distress and need. They were hungry, thirsty, strangers, naked, sick, and in prison. Such needs, acute and multiplied cannot be hidden. The fruits of the Holy Spirit are kindness, gentleness, sympathy, affection, helpfulness, and love. It is the love of Christ working through eyes, ears, hands, heart, and feet — going in search of him, hastening to embrace him, as he wanders through the bleak and cheerless city.

6. *Weekday Bible studies.* — In addition the church has twenty-six weekday Bible study classes and groups. These are correlated and guided by the Sunday School extension activities director.

Visitation Strongly Emphasized

A strong, vital, and vigorous visitation program is essential to a continuous growth of any Sunday School. The Sunday School of Curtis Baptist Church for the last thirteen years under the leadership of Dr. Bradley has excelled in a variety of programs, yet none more successful in its own right than visitation. The underlying cause for "a better than average" visitation program is the realization that "a great Sunday School doesn't just happen; you make it happen." The divine commission is found in Jesus' words, "Go ye therefore, and teach all nations, baptizing them in the name of the Father, and of the Son, and of the Holy Ghost: teaching them to observe all things whatsoever I have commanded you: and, lo, I am with you alway, even unto the end of the world." The Curtis purpose has been and is to create the atmosphere where the spirit of this commission can be carried out.

An up-to-date prospect file is maintained containing between four hundred and six hundred names. This is the first, if not the greatest asset in creating the possibility of a continuous growth. "We know 'who' is the prospect, 'where' to find them, and 'what' the spiritual need is."

During the last decade, as everywhere else, the population in the Greater Savannah River Area has shown a remarkable increase.

Curtis Church has kept abreast of this growth by extending a warm, compassionate, and friendly welcome to newcomers. Because of the presence, Fort Gordon, a nearby military base, and of the Medical College of Georgia, there is a turnover of families in the area. New industrial complexes are being located in the area which also means new arrivals. The church, therefore, must have an accelerated program.

It uses, not one, but a variety of methods in acquiring names of prospects.

(1) Names of newcomers are secured from the monthly utility magazine.

(2) Church members recommend new neighbors in their subdivisions.

(3) Visitors in Sunday School and worship services become choice prospects the first time they visit.

(4) Families inquiring and filing application to enroll children in the Curtis Christian School become fresh prospects.

(5) Children attending Vacation Bible School have opened a way of reaching people.

(6) The Bus Ministry affords a prime opportunity for reaching hundreds who otherwise would never be touched.

(7) Referrals are a unique way of discovering prospects. Church members tell the church of friends and relatives. Often a dedicated former member who has moved from Augusta, recommends the church to someone moving to the city.

(8) Crisis situation opens ways of ministering and at the same time ways of reaching many individuals for the Lord.

(9) Premarital counseling is a means of reaching individuals.

(10) Surveys of specific areas are productive (People Search).

The ultimate objective of the visitation program goes beyond adding names to a "prospect file." Acquiring the names for prospects is no major problem. There are people, people, people everywhere. The ultimate purpose is to follow up and enlist the prospects whose names are added.

This the church does, again not by a single plan but by a variety of plans. During the last several years a number of such approaches have been used.

(1) Numerous campaigns are promoted:

"Go and Tell"
"One for One"
Operation Fellowship
Crown Him King
Project Buddy System
Company of the Committed
Operation Personal Involvement
Adult Thrust
Committee of 100

(2) Departmental outreach leaders involve every Sunday School member.

(3) Teams of visitors go out weekly.

(4) Districts are covered. Visitors living in an area visit prospects within the area.

(5) Prayer breakfasts.

(6) Pastor's Guests.

(7) Deacon Involvement.

(8) Specials:

Revival. More than three hundred people committed themselves to visit a prospect during a week of Revival.

Rally.

(9) Ladies Day. Visitation is promoted by the ladies, including WMU.

(10) Mailouts. Prospect cards are mailed to visiting teams weekly. They visit and return cards with the results.

(11) Top Ten.

The key to the success of Curtis' Sunday School Growth with regards to the visitation program has come about exclusively because of the dedication of the membership to fulfill the mission given them by God — "Go and tell." They have gone and are presently going every day in search of new citizens for God's Kingdom.

Excellent and Adequate Buildings

One of the laws of Sunday School growth is that the buildings set the pattern. This, of course, is true only when other laws of growth are used and followed. The years following building expansions have shown marked growth.

The Sunday School enrollment in 1960 was 1,010 with an average attendance of 479. In 1961 the church lower auditorium was renovated and some other changes made. This made possible an enlargement of adult work from three to five departments, with addition of new classes. In 1962 the Sunday School enrollment grew to 1,525 and the attendance level rose to 709.

By 1963 enrollment had grown to 1,780 with an average attendance of 786. In 1964 the Bradley Building was constructed and ten new departments were begun. In the following year the enrollment advanced to 2,162 and attendance to 916.

By 1969 enrollment had grown to 2,298. Since the buildings were filled, average attendance had dropped slightly to 832. The Day Care Building was constructed at a cost of $180,000, and ten new departments were begun in 1970. By 1971 the Sunday School enrollment had grown to 3,290 and the average attendance rose to a new level of 1,162.

In 1972 two portable classroom buildings were purchased. The outreach ministry of the church was enlarged because of the acquisition of the "Chapel on Wheels." The bus ministry, which will be elaborated on later, was enlarged and the Sunday School experienced another surge of growth to an enrollment in 1973 of 3,609 with an average attendance of 1,389. By the fall of 1973 the attendance level rose to approximately 1,450.

All of this would have been hampered except for the vision demonstrated in acquiring expensive but necessary property. In the past thirteen years the church has purchased property valued at $750,000 to be used for parking.

Two other buildings have been built which add to parts of the ministry of the church. The gymnasium was built in 1964 and the high school building was used for the first time in the fall of 1973.

In 1972 the church engaged in an extensive renovation of the sanctuary. It is now one of the most beautiful places of worship in Augusta. The pastor does not say that the building was the reason for an upsurge in evangelism that year, but believes it helped in some ways. The year following (1973) he baptized 331 persons and saw a total of 539 people unite with the church. The final phase of that program was the purchase of a Schantz pipe organ at the cost of $80,000. The benefits in evangelism and a stronger desire to worship make it all worthwhile.

The church has invested $2,107,095 in new property, buildings, and equipment in the past thirteen years. The total value of the church property is now $3,322,075. And yet there is a desire to keep moving onward and upward.

The point needs to be made that Curtis has not built buildings and depended upon them to produce growth, but has sought people and built buildings to care for its expanding Sunday School.

Bus Ministry

For a number of years Curtis Church ministered on a limited basis through the use of one or two buses. In the main, this ministry was limited to elderly people. A tragedy in the city, however, brought about a new concern, especially on the part of the pastor.

Four youngsters were drowned. Because one of the boys had professed his faith in Christ at Curtis Church through the bus ministry, Dr. Bradley went to minister to the family. He was asked to conduct the service for all the boys because the other three families had no church affiliation.

Three out of four boys were lost because someone had failed.

Immediately following this incident, Dr. Bradley challenged the church to a new emphasis on bus ministry. It became a growing area of work.

In November, 1971, a full-time bus minister was added to the church staff, the first in Georgia. The bus workers reach into about four hundred homes each week and between two hundred and three hundred ride buses to Sunday School each Lord's Day.

In some churches bus outreach is responsible almost solely for an experience of growth. This is not true in Curtis. The bus program is done well, so well that the pastor appears regularly in bus conferences across the nation. Yet, the Sunday School grows in other ways also. The use of buses is one factor for growth, even a major factor, but not the only one. The strength of Curtis is greater than this.

Other Ministries

The full story of Curtis Baptist Church could not be told without a mention of the Day Care Center, the Curtis Elementary School, and Curtis High School. These ministries have developed across a number of years because of the concern of the church for children and youth and for working parents of preschoolers.

These, too, are considered to be a part of the outreach of the church. Every family member touched by one of these ministries potentially becomes a prospect for the Bible study program. The love and the concern of Curtis Church will be extended. The schools and related ministries are opportunities for direct service in their own right; they open other doors for the discovery of needs to which the church can minister.

Summary

The Sunday School of the Curtis Baptist Church indeed is one of the fastest growing. An adequate explanation for its growth may be found in Lawrence Bradley's words:

"So often a church that is genuinely concerned about people is accused of worshiping 'numbers.' In all honesty we admit that we enjoy the kind of success that can be shown statistically. But without a compassion which compels us to reach out, this 'numbers game' would leave an empty heart. We recognize that numbers are people and we are concerned.

"But as we reach out for more people, we also reach for better teaching. We insist on quality. There is no conflict between quality and quantity except that which is imposed by someone who accepts mediocrity. The continuous growth pattern shown by the Curtis Church is a testimonial to the long-lasting benefits of doing good work.

"Curtis has been and is a church with purpose: to reach out, to make disciples, to teach, to train, and to minister for the glory of God!"

9

Proclaiming the Word in Reaching People

North Phoenix Baptist Church
Phoenix, Arizona

The North Phoenix Baptist Church, Phoenix, Arizona, exemplifies what may happen when a people with a vision join hands with a pastor committed wholly to being used of God in growing and building a great church. The church has been described as achieving an impossible dream, the dream of reaching growing numbers of people for Bible study in one of the "pioneer areas" of Southern Baptists.

The church has had strong leadership in the early sixties and vision to believe that churches in the pioneer areas did not, of necessity, remain small and struggling. The people had a real conviction that the Lord needed a church in this area that had a large membership and could therefore get the attention of the community.

Because of that conviction, the church moved, in 1965, to a new location and constructed a new plant at a cost of approximately $1,000,000. The new facility would handle approximately 1,000 people in Bible study and provided an auditorium to care for an equal number. The choir area and additional space in the transepts of the auditorium increased the actual capacity to approximately 2,000. The church moved here and had its best years in 1965-66, averaging without its missions, in the neighborhood of 600 in Bible study.

Then, some problems which arose in the spring of 1967 brought an exodus of people. The pastor resigned and went to another place of service. In the spring of 1967, the Sunday School maintained an average of about 400.

In September, 1967, the average attendance, including missions, was 470; without the missions 400 or less.

The ministry of Richard Jackson began November 1, 1967. He came to the church from First Baptist Church, Sulphur Springs, Texas.

Like the church, Jackson had a vision of building and growing a great church in the city of Phoenix. He is the son of a pastor, Carroll Jackson, now retired after having served many years as a pastor of various churches in Texas. Jackson was saved at an early age, surrendered to the ministry, and received his education at Howard Payne College, Brownwood, Texas, and at Southwestern Baptist Theological Seminary, Fort Worth, Texas.

When he came to the church, he found conditions somewhat critical. The people still had the vision to move and build a great church for the Lord; however, problems needed to be solved. Circumstances in the sale of a previous property, not receiving moneys as expected, the church had gotten into arrears in its own payments. Without pastoral leadership, the church made a bond issue in the summer of 1967 to refinance its debt and to make the payments low enough for the church to handle.

The total income of the church in the first ten months of 1967 was $90,000.

"We started in November, 1967, with the standard approach to a Southern Baptist program," says the pastor. "We majored upon Bible study attendance, increasing the quality of Church Training, and a visitation program."

"We basically cleared the calendar of many other activities, excepting those that related specifically and positively to objectives. Sunday morning, Sunday evening, Wednesday evening, and prospect visitation day constituted the basic program of the church.

These emphases have continued to constitute the church program until now. There has been a broad emphasis upon the ministry of the Word. Jackson believes the ministry of the Word basically in three areas: proclamation, teaching, and sharing through personal witnessing.

Jackson feels it to be his burden and his call to preach the Bible and to make that his business. He preaches expository sermons, trying always to ask God to help him have the element of teaching, as well as the prophetic element in his preaching.

Secondly, there is the ministry of teaching the Word, which includes the Sunday School where the Bible is taught.

Then there is the ministry of sharing through personal witnessing, this obviously is the responsibility of every Christian wherever he may be found. With this emphasis the church began to grow steadily. During the church year, 1967-68, it baptized 206 people. This was with no revival meeting as such.

In the six years Jackson has been pastor of North Phoenix, the church has had only one "revival meeting," eight days long. That was with a good evangelist and was a good meeting, but it did not seem to add to the numbers that were reached, and it also took away from some other things upon which the church was placing an emphasis. The church has had no other such meeting, not that Jackson is against them, they just do not seem to be best for his ministry at this time.

The church continues to grow. Our Sunday School emphasis was upon growth. No sign-up campaign. Regular emphasis upon Bible study.

"We do have the regular Southern Baptist organization," says Jackson. "At periodic times — almost once a year now — we conduct a Sunday School enlargement campaign, occasionally introducing a variation here and there, but basically our Sunday School has been built upon standard Southern Baptist methods. We use Flake's five points. We just have the standard Southern Baptist approach, almost exclusively."

The Sunday School has grown steadily; there never has been a Miracle Sunday or a sign-up campaign or a large attendance day. At the end of six years of Jackson's pastorate, the church has baptized more than 2,000 people with 70 percent of these being eighteen years of age or over. This is without a revival meeting and without a bus ministry. He feels both of these are good ministries; they just are not for his situation at the present time. During this period the church has had total additions of about 4,000, a net increase has been shown of some 3,000 people. This means that the church maintains a relationship of some kind to three out of four of those who are added to its membership.

To understand this growth, it is important to know that the church is not in "Sunday School territory." The highest attendance figures reached by the Sunday School have been over 1,800, but the preaching attendance Sunday-by-Sunday is almost twice as much. The church televises its morning worship services over statewide color live television. It owns the equipment. This is a significant part of the church's program.

The educational space of the church cares for about 1,700, and that is the range within which the Sunday School attendance figures at the present time. This illustrates, as the pastor says, one of the laws of growth as stated by J. N. Barnette. A church cannot grow beyond its space. Jackson believes that the Sunday School cannot go to two Sunday Schools because of limitations on parking. The type buildings the church has provides a great amount of adult space and this is connected to the auditorium. For these reasons, a double Sunday School seems to be not feasible at the present time.

In 1972 some of the men of the church uncovered the possibility of purchasing forty acres of land just south of the present location of the church. This is the only large tract of land in the central Phoenix corridor which has never been developed, having been a part of an estate. The church voted to purchase this property at a price of $2,000,000 and immediately raised over $200,000 above the budget for a down payment. Payment is arranged in the budget for the coming year and further payments will be divided in this manner. Architects are now developing plans for the first phase development. There is to be an auditorium which will seat 4,000 people, educational space for 3,500 to 4,000 people, with the possibility of enlargement in the future, a chapel, and an activities building, and a plan for full development of the forty acres. Landscaping is provided to allow for later additions to the buildings themselves.

The present facilities must be expanded in the meantime. The church cannot move to the new property for from two to three years, no matter how fast plans are completed. The pastor feels the church must continue to grow during the time it takes the new facilities to be completed. In view of the fact that the present space is saturated, the church is making plans to add one more educational unit to the present complex. This will take away some of the present parking space, so the church is planning to park people on the new property and bus them to the present facility. Indeed, it already is doing this.

The projected educational unit on the present property will handle approximately 700 people and permit the church to develop its Sunday School to between 2,000 and 2,500 in attendance. This will give time to build the new buildings on the new location.

Sunday night attendance at North Phoenix overflows the 2,000 seat auditorium. Every Sunday night sees a capacity crowd. The Wednesday night attendance now is higher than Sunday morning worship attendance was less than five years ago. Emphasis here is upon prayer and Bible study.

The major visitation thrust is on Monday; however, a couple of other visitation efforts are made during each week.

"I probably ought to say something about the staff," says Jackson. "When I came, I was the only male full time member on the staff. There were a couple of secretaries and a part-time bookkeeper. We do not have a large staff. There are now four other full-time vocational ministers. We're adding a fifth, a genuine minister of outreach. He will not be a glorified visitation captain; he will be to the outreach organization of the Sunday School what the minister of education is to the teaching organization. He will have the responsibility to staff and lead the outreach force throughout the Bible study program. He will maintain a full staff of outreach people just as a full staff of teachers is maintained. He will have certain other responsibilities in some areas, providing prospects, assuming custodianship of records, preparing materials and conducting evangelistic Bible study, and whatever else he can do to help people in reaching people.

The baptismal record of the church over the years reflects evangelistic concern at the present time. In 1968 the church baptized 250 people; in 1968-69, 265 people; in 1969-70, 357 people; in 1970-71, 411 people; and in 1971-72, 433 people. The baptismal record for 1973-74 will be even higher. In this period additions to the church have been in 1973, 853 people; in 1972, 860 people; and in 1971, 830 people.

Are there areas where the church has placed special emphasis in its efforts to reach people? There are. Jackson tells about these.

"When we first came to Phoenix, we recognized that there was a wealth of prospects in the young married adult area, from marriage to about thirty years of age. Therefore, we developed an approach aimed at these young adults which combined the best we thought we found in a couple of things. We felt the couples class idea had some good even though we recognized the dangers of such an approach. We recognized, also, the wisdom of using proven Southern Baptist methods. Combining these two, we started a Young Adult department. We used a fine Bible teacher to do a thirty-minute lecture, then organized into classes for discussion. We use a discussion leader, who is responsible not only for activities in the classroom situation but for contacting and ministering to all persons in his organization, that is in the small unit." How well has this plan worked? The church now has four of these departments where it had only one in the beginning. The people have done a tremendous job in reaching young adults.

Another area in which the church has placed a special emphasis is single young adults. The pastor tells how the church became concerned for this age group.

"A single young lady brought me a booklet entitled "The Church Is Driving Me to Drink." It was written by a man who placed himself in the position of a divorced man. The booklet described the situation of the single adult. The writer said that he seemed to fit nowhere; he had no place to go. This described the situation of single adults in their "thirties." The only place they could go for companionship was to bars and to dance studios. We became concerned about the fact that single adults, whether never married or whether divorced, just seemed to fit nowhere. So we started a single adult department."

How well has this approach succeeded? The church now has four large single adult departments. Attendance in these departments ranges from 200 to more than 300 Sunday by Sunday. The pastor has baptized numbers of people from these departments. He has also seen homes put back together and has seen many lives salvaged when they seemed beyond redemption.

How does Jackson explain his ministry?

"Basically, we have attempted to reproduce our burden in laymen," he answers. "We make a great use of Southern Baptist programs, such as the Forward Program of Church Finance. We modify it, but we use it. We use the Deacon-Led Spiritual Growth Program extensively. Our deacons are the spiritual ministers of the church, greatly used and greatly respected. I think we have good programs in our denomination and I've never been happier to be a

The attractive auditorium of the North Phoenix Baptist Church, Phoenix, Arizona.

The modern facilities of the North Phoenix Baptist Church.

Southern Baptist than now. We do the basic things, but we do them better."

"What if a man says to you that he does exactly the same thing and yet does not seem to succeed?" I asked Jackson. "How would you answer that person?"

"Don't ever think I'm leaving out the emphasis on the Holy Spirit," Jackson answered. "I believe the power of the Holy Spirit is the only power to build a church. I really zeroed in on my men and on reproducing my burden in them. And I pray for the ingenuity and spirituality to motivate them."

"And how do you motivate your people?" I asked.

"We don't motivate with campaigns and promotions, but with commitment to a great purpose," Jackson answered. "I take my cue from a statement I found in Bruce Barton's *The Man Nobody Knows*. Dr. Barton says that the major element of leadership is not charisma but that the No. 1 essential in leadership is an overwhelming sense of purpose and a complete commitment. That commitment expresses itself in the way a person works and leads. I think our people see this commitment in me. It is reproduced in the staff. They believe the work we're doing is the most important work on earth, and they communicate this feeling to the people. Our people feel they are indeed fortunate to be a part of this work."

"Another thing we try to do is to emphasize that the people should enjoy their salvation," Jackson continued. "I feel that one of the reasons people don't witness is because they don't have anything to share. Emphasize the positive joy of salvation, lead them to experience this joy, and they will have a joy to share with others."

Jackson thought for a moment and then continued answering the question about his success in leading North Phoenix Church. "When men ask me about my church, I look at them and say: 'Look, you probably can preach as good as I can. I know you can study your Bible. Now the main thing to do is just to have such an overwhelming commitment to the thing yourself that your people catch it.' Quite frankly, I'm committed to building a great church, to building it solid and strong. To build it so, I've had to readjust my thinking to the fact that God wants me to build a church, a great church, a church that is reaching people, in Phoenix, Arizona. God has not called me to build it just big enough to open other opportunities to me, that is, opportunities to go to bigger churches, but God has called me to build a church here to his glory. I think my people know that I am committed that way. The thing that motivates people is that they can see in you as their leader this overwhelming commitment. Basic commitment to the work you are doing. I know God has given me gifts, and I'm grateful for these gifts, but my basic commitment is the secret of my life."

10

Involving Church People in Reaching People

Eastwood Baptist Church
Tulsa, Oklahoma

Eastwood Baptist Church of Tulsa, Oklahoma, first met May 1, 1955, with 35 people present. It was constituted June 4, 1956, and with 247 members. On the day it was constituted 159 attended Sunday School and 79 Training Union. Since then the church has had four full-time pastors: Jim Austin, Howard Kilb, Kenneth Mullins, who is now with the Stewardship Commission, and Tom Elliff, the present pastor.

The present Sunday School enrollment is 2,114 and attendance level averaging above 1,100. Church in Training enrollment is 680 with an attendance level nearing 500. The music program has 720 people enrolled, with about 485 in music attendance each week. The Sunday School enrollment has increased at an average about 100 a year since the constitution of the church.

Under the leadership of the present pastor, Tom Elliff, who came as pastor in August, 1972, Eastwood Church is experiencing rapid growth on the premise that people are hungry for sound Bible teaching without compromise. The church leadership emphasizes the fact that the church is teaching the Word of God and the pastor often reminds the congregation that the Bible reveals both the contents and the direction for the abundant life. "If you change the contents or refuse to follow the directions, you can't have what God promised you," Elliff says.

During September, 1972, the Eastwood Sunday School underwent some major changes. At that time, records revealed that a total of 1,522 people were enrolled in Sunday School, and the average attendance during that month was 701. The Sunday School has grown steadily, yet not rapidly during the seventeen-year history of the church. Still, the church leaders feel an urgency of winning Tulsa for Christ before his coming. This feeling motivates the program of the church. "What is his plan for reaching Tulsa for

Christ?" was the one question asked from the church floor as the church considered extending a call to Elliff. For years the church has felt this to be their responsibility.

In October, 1972, Eastwood published *Division '73*, which was a part of a book, related to the church stewardship campaign. Included in this publication was a presentation of the church goals and programs for the coming year. The Sunday School goal was to enroll 2,000 in Bible study with an average attendance of 1,000. But by October, 1973, about a year later, records showed 2,114 enrolled in Bible study and an attendance level of 1,033. These figures represent only the enrollment and attendance on Sunday; they do not include the fifteen weekday Bible study fellowships groups which function under the leadership of many church members.

Several important factors have contributed to the growth of Eastwood's Bible teaching program — leadership commitment, visitation, teacher preparation, effective Sunday morning presentation, and family-centered programing.

Leadership Commitment

No Sunday School can rise above the commitment of its leadership. In a letter to the Sunday School leaders, the pastor made a stirring challenge. "Help make Eastwood the greatest Bible teaching church in the Southwest," he said. "The souls of men and women, boys and girls are at stake. They can be reached and you can reach and teach them, but it will require unusual dedication. Now concerning your place of responsibility, I fully believe you have your responsibility because God has called you into his service and not because the church drafted you. This being the case, I'm confident that your heart's desire is to fulfill your responsibility joyfully, willingly, and effectively. Enclosed is a schedule of weekly activities in which you will be directly involved. Now, I realize that for a precious few individuals participation in all of these activities might be difficult or even impossible because of extenuating circumstances — your job or your health, for instance. But, under God, I think it is imperative to attend these functions if at all possible. For a teacher or an officer deliberately to be absent from these activities is to set the poorest possible example. To stay away on Sunday or Wednesday evening simply because it's your night out or you don't want to come when something is good on television is not an extenuating circumstance. It is the same as saying to your class members one hour is enough each week for me to grow spiritually. Friend, if you don't attend a class where you're being taught, why should your class members. What I'm asking you to do is this, examine your intentions for the coming year; if you know right now that you will not be coming to teachers and officers' meetings, to Wednesday visitation night, and to both Sunday services and your inability is not caused by either job, health, or other extenuating circumstances, I prayerfully encourage you to allow somebody else to take your responsibility. If you will not be serving, call us soon so provisions may be made. If we do not hear from you, we will fully expect your presence at each of these activities throughout the year. I am praying for you personally, trusting God to give you great victories in your place of service this year."

The church takes attendance records at the meetings of which the pastor speaks: on visitation night, officers and teachers' meeting, and of course on Sunday morning. The record is published twice a year for all to see the attendance of teachers and officers at Eastwood at these different meetings. This is done at a banquet, and we ask for folks at the banquet to pray for those who are attending less than 50 percent of the time.

It was felt that there were some inadequacies in the annual nomination of teachers and officers and feared that many people would accept the responsibility because it was only for a year anyway, and others who discovered that they were out of place would just hang in there until the first Sunday in October. In either case, some leadership positions were occupied by individuals who were not really committed to the task. Many churches have seen the annual selection as a good way to get rid of bad teachers, but Eastwood's leadership sees this as simply a refusal to act honestly with the teachers and to accept the responsibility of leadership. Wrong teachers can damage permanently the class in only a few weeks not to mention several months. So teachers were notified of the new nature of their responsibility, that is, that they were selected on a permanent basis, and they were informed that when difficulties seemed apparent the staff would willingly meet with them to work things out in a suitable way. This might involve prayer, personal counseling, or the staff might encourage a teacher to allow someone else to assume his responsibility until he could devote the needed amount of them. If the attendance of a teacher at the meeting does fall off, the staff approaches him to determine whether a problem exists which might be solved. "We wonder if you need some help in there?" the staff member asks. "Would you like someone to take your place until you get things worked out?" Nobody has become angered or caused a problem.

A permanent record is kept on the Sunday School worker's attendance on Sunday morning and teachers and officers' meeting on Sunday evening and visitation on Wednesday evening. This record is periodically reviewed to maintain an awareness of potential trouble spots or weaknesses in Bible teaching staff.

"Our school teachers and officers now number approximately 210," says Elliff. "That's a ratio of one to ten enrolled for each worker."

If the pastor and church could have their way, it would be smaller than that. "We feel we need thirty teachers right now," the pastor pointed out. "I certainly don't think you could grow with a bigger ratio."

Visitation

Eastwood leadership believes that the Sunday School will not grow consistently without an organized visitation program. If visitation is that important, the church ought to schedule it on important nights. It was this feeling that motivated the change to Wednesday evening for visitation.

For one hour after fellowship supper and before the Bible teaching service, teachers and officers and class members visit in the homes of prospective members and absentees. The emphasis is on the number of people out visiting rather than the number of visits made. Currently over a hundred people each week visit during this hour.

The pastor and staff led the people to set some goals as to how many people they wanted out visiting. These and other goals relating to the Sunday are set at semiannual Sunday School leadership banquets. Prior to the Wednesday visitation, however, every teacher and officer receives a Sunday School newsletter. It consists of two pages, one page used for general promotion, prepared by Howard Waller, Minister of Education, and the second page containing the name and address, department, and teacher responsible for everyone who the previous Sunday visited in Sunday School or in one of the worship services and everyone who the previous week joined the church. Teachers are encouraged to contact every visitor before Saturday of each week. The real emphasis is placed upon the "before Saturday."

On Saturday two additional groups supplement the Sunday School visitation. First of all, approximately forty individuals visit for the bus ministry, which brings in about 250 individuals to Bible study each week. And Eastwood's staff counts Saturday as a complete workday, for everybody on the staff visits all day every Saturday. The staff meets at 9:00 in the morning, has doughnuts and milk with the bus people, and then go out to visit all day. The staff members attempt to visit in the home of every person who visited the church the previous week. Sometimes this numbers from seventy to one hundred visits they must make on that one day. More often than not the home already has been visited by a Sunday School worker. Usually a letter has gone out. The letter and two visits during the week brings most visitors back a second Sunday.

Teacher Preparation

Eastwood's officers and teachers' meeting is considered a must for an effective Sunday presentation of the Bible. This meeting is held in conjunction with other training programs on Sunday evenings. The first fifteen minutes of the hour-long sessions are given to a general assembly of all officers and teachers and this is a time of information, motivation, and inspiration. This period is under the leadership of the Sunday School director. His name is Louis Blosch and Louis has been Sunday School director for about three years. He is an insurance salesman, but his pastor describes him as "just a fantastic Sunday School director." He seems to serve on the staff in a volunteer way as much as a minister of education might.

After this general session forty-five minutes are given to review and to preparation for the coming week. Some people believe

enlisted in the fall of 1972, and the six chairmen participated in a training school for lay evangelism leaders in Dallas on November 14, 1972. There they received guidance for a more thorough preparation of the school in the home church.

Special witnessing Sunday School lessons were in the youth and adult divisions and five Bible search programs were presented in Training Union prior to the school. Dr. Leavell directed his preaching program toward personal involvement in witnessing. Prayer saturated all preparation activities.

Mr. Stricklin requested that all sessions be conducted in the fellowship hall and gym area for informality and ease in group study. Preenrollment assured a large school, but when it got under way 497 were present. On Wednesday evening during the school, all other activities were suspended and nearly 400 church members scattered over the city to share the love of Christ. When they reported back to the church, they reported 52 people saved and much renewal in the lives of backslidden Christians.

Not only was this the largest lay evangelism school to be reported in the Southern Baptist Convention, but there is a continuing interest in witnessing in the church. Something happened to the church and keeps on happening. The church now has over 400 youth and adults who are "not ashamed of the gospel" and who aggressivley tell the story of what Christ has done for them and what he will do for anyone who accepts him.

Dual Sunday School

Made necessary by the rapid growth of the Sunday School, in May, 1973 a dual Sunday School was put into effect. Melvin Bradley, minister of education, worked out the details of the plan to provide necessary space. Sunday Schools begin at 9:30 and 11:00 with dual worship services in the church auditorium at the same times. Graded children's worship services also are scheduled to conform to the Sunday School program.

These dual Sunday Schools are a matter of expediency because of lack of space; they will be abandoned when additional property makes it possible to go back to one Sunday School.

Future Children's Building

On July 23, 1973, the church voted to purchase the Wichita

Falls Clinic Hospital property across the street from the church. This 38,000 square foot structure is to be vacated early in 1974 at which time an extensive remodeling and renovation program is planned by the church. The new facilities will accommodate grades one through six. It has 114 paved parking spaces ready for use by the church.

The completion of plans for this building will make possible going back to one Sunday School.

Visitation

Visitation receives a major emphasis in the church. Two weeks of each month are designated as visitation weeks. On these weeks no major activity other than visitation may be planned. The church calendar is set up with one week a red week and one week a green week. The green week means to go, go for visitation. "Just for the sake of change for a time we made the red week the week to go," the pastor says. "But this demonstrates that the heart of our outreach is zeroing in on visitation."

Each of the adult classes and the other departments of the Sunday School have outreach leaders. They are basically responsible for getting at least one representative of their units present for visitation.

Even though all the green week is given to visitation, one day is especially designated on this week. On this day every class and department, as nearly as possible, has at least one person present for the work. Specific visitation assignments are made and definite reports are expected.

Church Recreation

Church recreation serves a dual purpose of outreach and the building of fellowship within the church family. The First Baptist Church maintains a year-round systematic recreation program for young and old alike, under the leadership of Howard Chapman, director of children's education, activities, and recreation.

The recreation-activities building, completed in 1968 includes recreational facilities equalled by few churches anywhere. A high school size gymnasium is a multi-purpose area. When space is needed movable partitions bring it into the fellowship hall. Its banquet capacity is six hundred. A modern kitchen backs up the banquet hall. There is also a snack bar in the recreation area. The latter is used regularly by the church staff and by members who drop in for a workout or who simply want a quick lunch in the friendly atmosphere of the church.

Use of the gymnasium facilities is restricted to certain hours for the different age groups and for organized competition. The gym is used also for roller skating, with the skates available there.

Six regulation bowling lanes, two billiard tables, and two ping-pong tables are available at designated hours. Opening off the game area is a craft room in which equipment is available for several handicrafts.

The kitchen and snack bar serve some forty thousand meals a year, according to the best estimates. Among the regularly scheduled events catered to are the family night suppers on Wednesdays, lunch and dinner on visitation days, and the monthly meetings of the Woman's Missionary Union. Snacks are served the chapel choir on Sunday evenings and noon meals are served from the snack bar at all times except visitation days.

International Friends Group

Ride one of the First Baptist buses on Sunday morning. At the first stop the bus captain steps off to greet two small children, an eight-year-old girl holding the hand of her six-year-old brother. The bus captain — or bus pastor — steps back on the bus, the driver pulls the door closed and the bus moves on to the next stop. Here the first stop is almost repeated, but at the third stop a woman enters the bus with her five-year-old. She is Oriental in appearance. Several times this is repeated until by the time the bus is filled and starts its return trip to the church six or eight women are riding. These, in appearance, may be Japanese, Spanish, or some other nationality. They are riding the bus — and many of them have been won to Christ and church membership — as a result of work done by the International Friends Group with the support of Sunday School classes and departments and the bus program itself.

This work was begun in 1968. At first it was an effort aimed at an informal teaching of English to women transplanted in Wichita Falls from their own countries, but the genuine friendship of the volunteers from the Woman's Missionary Union, which undertook the project, soon made it clear that lessons would be blended with spontaneous friendship.

The first year's enrollment was about forty women from Germany, Cuba, Czechoslovakia, Korea, Japan, Italy, Spain, Ecuador, Libya, and Venezuela. Since then students have been welcomed also from Greece, Russia, Taiwan, Thailand, Vietnam, Okinawa, the Philippines, Mexico, Nepal, Hungary, and Panama.

The women, most of whom are married to Americans they met overseas or are the wives of foreign students, have learned to speak English, read and write the language, learned about citizenship, taken driver's education, studied first aid, and worked on crafts.

Two buses bring them in from Sheppard Field to the week-day meetings of the International Friends Group. This increased attendance dramatically, even makes it possible for some to attend at all, for transportation is a problem for many of them.

As a part of the Sunday School an international Bible class is provided for them on Sunday morning. This opens up the possibility of witnessing to them as class members. Many of the group have been won to Christ.

Television Ministry

The church was introduced on television June 4, 1961. The worship service was first televised June 6, 1971. The church owns two color television cameras. Surveys have indicated that as many as twenty thousand people view the broadcast of the Sunday morning service each week. This has become a major factor in the outreach program of the church.

Good Administration

One of the essentials to the growth of a Sunday School is good administration of the organization so that many people are involved, with each performing his assigned task to the best of his ability. This involves planning, training, and constant attention to details. Dr. Leavell gives great credit to his staff which does this work. Key man here is Melvin Bradley, the minister of education. He works with the staff people and with the volunteer leaders of the teachers and officers of the Sunday School, of which there are more than four hundred.

Guided by a Purpose

When asked to detail or outline the steps taken to achieve growth in the Sunday School, Dr. Leavell thinks for a minute. He speaks of some or all the things listed here. Then he tells the story of how the growth pattern began. Finally, he stops to think of what he has said.

"Actually, these were not parts of an outline," he says. "We just made the initial commitment, then all these other decisions followed as a matter of course."

The initial commitment to reach people sets the course of a church and determines the priorities it will set.

12

Growing a Country Church for Reaching People

Amite Baptist Church
Denham Springs, Louisiana

Amite Baptist Church, Denham Springs, Louisiana — according to *The Quarterly Review,* a publication of The Sunday School Board of the Southern Baptist Convention — is the fourth largest rural church in the entire Southern Baptist Convention. It is located near Baton Rouge, Louisiana's capital city, four miles from the town of Denham Springs.

The industrialization of the Baton Rouge area has brought many people to the community and helped to create a climate for church growth, most of which has taken place in the last twenty years. The most rapid growth, however, has come about in the last six years. In 1967 Sunday School enrollment was 734 and the average weekly attendance was 345. The grand total membership then was 958. In 1970 the average Sunday School attendance was 385; in 1973 it had climbed to 550. The enrollment had increased to 1,139. Similarly the total membership of the church has climbed to more than 1,400.

During this same six year period — 1967 to 1973 — the church's financial receipts increased from $108,000 to $154,000 and mission giving from $23,000 to more than $30,000. Church property values increased during this same period almost $250,000 largely due to the construction of a new building. Perhaps the point at which the rate of growth of this aggressive church can most clearly be seen is in number of baptisms. A look at the records reveals only 133 for the period 1962 through 1966 while 406 were baptized during the six years just ending.

Early History

The first Baptist church known to be organized in the state of Louisiana was the Half Moon Bluff Church, organized on October 12, 1812. Not many years later the Amite Baptist Church came into being near Denham Springs. Its constitution as a Baptist church is recorded as October 9, 1841. Through Christ's guidance, the sacrifice and hard work of the members has brought continual physical and spiritual growth to the church.

Rev. W. D. Allen was pastor of the church from the time of its organization but was called officially on December 8, 1843. He arrived in Amite community when a young man, bought a section of land, and planted his life here. There is no record of the meager salary he received. He earned a living from his farm and preached the gospel one Sunday a month at Amite church. He rode long distances on horseback to preach to other churches when practically the only roads were trails made by bear hunters.

He baptized 142 people into the fellowship of Amite Church, received 95 by letter, and eight were restored while he was pastor. For thirty-four years he served as moderator of the Eastern Louisiana Association. The Amite Church during this time led the association in gifts to associational and denominational causes. At his death church membership numbered 118.

Both the church and the association passed resolutions praising his life and work.

The present building faces the cemetery just across the road where a monument has been erected over his grave by the Eastern Louisiana Association, Amite Church, relatives, and friends in memory of the pastor who was with them from the beginning and who led the church successfully through the period of the Civil War and the trying days that followed.

In February, 1843, a committee was appointed to receive a title for land which was to be given to the church. They apparently did not get a clear title to this land for in 1856 the church appointed another committee to select land and see about building a meeting house. A title to the land was received in May, 1856, and the first building erected.

In August, 1862, the Federal Army visited and injured the church building, so that people were unable to have church either Saturday or Sunday.

In January, 1872, a plot of land was bought and a building erected which was used for worship until the house was blown down by wind and destroyed in 1879. The site of this building was in the lot now occupied by the church cemetery. A second building erected on part of this lot in 1885 was under the leadership of Rev. J. T. Ott. The little white church was erected on this site in 1914 under the leadership of pastor H. T. Comish.

In 1935 the annex was added and a few years later the building was again remodeled. In 1933 under the leadership of Rev. J. E. Chandler the first lighting system with a carbide plant was installed. This was replaced later by a Deko system.

The story of the present house of worship runs back to the years of 1942 and 1943 when the first building fund was started. Every member who was employed or had an income was asked to give a day's wages to the building fund. The date was set several weeks in advance and on that first offering more than $800 was given.

Easter Sunday, 1944, was a day to remember. A goal was set for fifteen additions to the church, 200 in Sunday School, 100 in Training Union, and $1,000 in offering for the building fund. The church received twelve additions, had an attendance of over 200 in Sunday School, 128 in Training Union, and in just six minutes the people brought $2,215 and placed it in a tub which had been decorated and placed on a table in front of the pulpit. This truly was the beginning of big things for the church.

The church had over $18,000 in the building fund when the foundation for the building was laid.

The educational wing of the church was completed in May, 1961, at a total cost of $70,000. In 1929 the first pastor's home was erected. Currently, the church owns two homes for occupancy by the pastor and associate pastor. The total church property includes over twenty acres with a total value (land and building) of over $650,000.

Amite Church has a history of a great spirit of Christian love and obedience to the will of God. The church believes that together under the leadership of the Holy Spirit she can do anything God may want her to do. This church has grown from a membership of 20 at the time of its organization to a present total of 1,384 but even at the present membership as compared to the beginning nucleus these numbers do not begin to tell the story of its growth. Across the years, hundreds upon hundreds of lives have been touched by the ministry of this great church.

A New Spirit in the Church

James K. Pierce became pastor of the church in 1962, about the time of his graduation from the New Orleans Baptist Theological Seminary. Pierce is a native of Corinth, Mississippi, and an honor graduate of Mississippi College. Prior to coming to Amite church, all his pastorates had been in the state of Mississippi. He serves on the Executive Board of the Louisiana Baptist Convention, on the board of trustees for the Southeastern Baptist Assembly, and a moderator of the Eastern Louisiana Baptist Association.

The 132-year-old church caught fire spiritually following a deacon's retreat. This was in 1966. The thrust of this retreat was pastoral ministry responsibilities of deacons and lay involvement. The idea caught on and the leadership began to see the potential of the church. They started praying for things to happen and began believing they would.

Some time later, for the first time in the history of the church, the Sunday School reached an attendance of 500. The pastor tells about this eventful day. "We set a goal of 500 for our Sunday School," he says. "For two or three weeks prior to the target date, as pastor, I took advantage of every opportunity to say to the church; We are going to have more than 500 in Sunday School on our High Attendance Day."

"The day came and the excitement started to build as the count came in. The number was totaled and showed we had 499. Just as everyone began to express disappointment over a number which was far above any previous high, a department secretary walked into the office saying he had a couple to come in late. "Add two more to our count," he said. This we did, not at all reluctantly, bringing our total to 501.

"A skeptical deacon said, 'Pastor, I never would have believed you but now I will never doubt you.'

"This positive approach became a matter of course. Sunday School workers are admonished never to speak negatively or even think that way. All church workers are reminded that God wants to do something truly great and wonderful through our church and he only waits for us to place our hands in his and walk with him. Failure and defeat are words that have no place in our church vocabulary. We really believe that faith is the victory that overcomes the world."

Amite Baptist Church, Denham Springs, Louisiana, is the fourth largest rural church in the Southern Baptist Convention.

Not content to maintain the "status quo" Amite Baptist Church enlarges through bus ministry.

The spirit of renewal caught the church; as spiritual growth took place, numerical increases followed. As Pierce describes the church, many factors come in for attention.

Involving many people. — "We seek also to involve as many of our members as possible in some type of church responsibility." The pastor says. "We have discovered that the more involved our people are, the happier they are and the more spiritual growth they experience. We believe the old adage 'A pulling horse won't kick and a kicking horse won't pull.' Lay involvement is the big thing with us because we truly believe that it is God's intention for everyone of his children to minister. Members are frequently reminded of what Paul said in Ephesians 2:10: 'For we are his workmanship, created in Christ Jesus unto good works, which God hath before ordained that we should walk in them.' "

Evangelism. — The primacy of evangelism is stressed. People are taught that since Jesus came to seek and to save that which was lost and since he charges his followers again and again to be witnesses unto him the main task is to bring people to him. The church believes its every activity is or should be for the ultimate purpose of bringing men to Jesus. Every program activity is judged on the basis of its effectiveness in reaching people for Christ.

Revivals. — Revivals receive priority positions on the church calendar because they are recognized as an effective means of bringing men to Christ. No expense is spared and every energy is expended in preparation. Amite has come to be a great revival church. "So much work goes into preparation that all the visiting preacher needs to do is stand to preach and then stand back to watch God move and the Holy Spirit work and the people respond," the pastor says with a smile.

Witness training. — From time to time personal soul-winning is taught and sermons are preached on the subject. The church has also held a lay evangelism school to equip the membership with soul-winning.

Visitation. — "A Sunday School grows in direct proportion to the number and quality of visits made," observed J. N. Barnette in justifying visitation as one of the seven laws of Sunday School growth. In the Amite church visitation is strongly emphasized. Members are constantly reminded that people are important to God and therefore should be important to the church.

Fellowship. — Fellowship is another big factor in the growth of a church. Although the congregation is fairly large, somehow the people have been able to maintain a friendly atmosphere and a strong spiritual fellowship. Time and again visitors have commented on the friendliness of the people and the strong spiritual atmosphere of the church. We encourage our people to get together on their own for fellowship experiences, and the church as often as possible has fellowship for all its members. The idea of the church as a family is promoted. People are encouraged to bear one another's burdens and to share each other's joy. Love for one another is an identifying characteristic of the members of this church. It is truly a church that cares.

A full and well-rounded program. — For many members the church is the center of almost all the family's activities. A full and well-rounded church program provides almost any kind of activity in which a person might have interest. For instance, for the recreation-minded family member, there are tennis courts and a gymnasium. For the person interested in music there is a fully graded choir program as well as other types of music activity. For the young person there are many kinds of activities, including summer retreats. For those interested in Bible study and mission study many opportunities for learning are offered. For those interested in helping others there are ministry opportunities open.

Bus Outreach

One of the greatest boons of all to the growth of Amite Church was the beginning of its bus ministry in October, 1971. This innovative program was begun only after much prayer and careful study. "I had read as much material as possible on the bus ministry which at the time was still in its infancy in Southern Baptist churches," Pierce recalls. "Being very impressed with the success other churches were experiencing in reaching people through this ministry I began praying for direction from God about trying to lead our church into this new type of outreach program. At the same time God was working through his Holy Spirit in the heart of one of our laymen who became burdened regarding our need for a trip bus."

This matter was presented to the church and a new bus was purchased. Shortly afterwards the church used the bus to bring in children for Vacation Bible School. On the first day the one bus was packed with ninety children. A second bus was located to finish out the week in Bible school. At the end of the week enrollment just jumped seven short of one hundred from the previous year. It had become evident that the church needed to be involved in bus outreach.

Therefore, the associate pastor was asked to attend a bus conference in another state and gather all information possible. Upon his return he shared his excitement and newly acquired knowledge with the pastor. Together they sat down and mapped out plans, a course of action, to find God's will for the church.

Again the pastor takes up the story. "I was to preach a sermon on bus outreach seeking to get the congregation behind the program," he says. "Already we had been talking to our leadership and convincing them. When the invitation was extended at the close of that bus ministry sermon, forty-six people pledged to give $100 each to buy two additional buses and over forty people pledged to work in the ministry in whatever capacity they might be needed. We were on the way."

The church purchased two additional buses and began on the first Sunday in October, 1971, with three buses. The church sets a high attendance goal for the first Sunday of each new Sunday School year; that year the goal was high because of launching the new bus ministry. The goal was 700. The Sunday School had 756; 223 of these were children who rode buses. It is difficult to describe the excitement this bus growth generated.

It became necessary to have two Sunday Schools and two worship services. Additional teachers and workers had to be found and space problems worked out. For sometime prior to the beginning of the bus ministry, the church had been talking about the need for more educational space but had not been able to get beyond the talking stage. Now something had to be done. The long-range planning committee set to work and some presented a recommendation for a combination education/recreation building.

Now, the new building is a reality. It contains 15,400 square feet of educational space and 6,300 square feet of recreational area. The educational unit houses ten Sunday School departments, eight of which were organized as new departments on July 1, 1973.

Not only did the bus outreach program increase attendance but it made the church more aware of the need for ministry in other ways and in other areas. The people became aware of the need for clothing, food, medical help, counseling needs, as well as other things. The congregation responded beautifully to these needs, and Sunday School departments and classes took upon themselves projects to provide the needed food, clothing, medical help, or whatever else might be needed. Our people always seemed willing; even anxious to help.

A story the pastor often tells in the bus conferences in which he now often participates epitomizes the meaning of the bus program and the reason Amite church pushes it to reach the last possible person.

"Not long after our ministry started, four-year-old Tonya began riding one of the buses." She was so excited from week to week as the bus captain came by each Saturday to visit and that the bus came by on Sunday to take her to church. One Saturday the bus captain went by to visit and found Tonya playing and excited as usual over his visit as well as the prospect of riding the bus the next day. That night Tonya's mother called her in for the evening meal, her bath, and to bed. The next morning the mother went in to wake Tonya. The little girl could not be aroused. She had died during the night of a congenital heart ailment.

"Because of Tonya's love for the church bus, her parents requested that the teenage bus assistants serve as pallbearers. She was buried in the church cemetery. Just a week or so later I buried Tonya's father and mother in beautiful baptism. It wasn't long then before the father was asking for a place to serve in the bus ministry. He became one of our bus captains.

"Many of our people who had not been involved in the work of the church became involved through the bus ministry. We have people serving as drivers, captains, mechanics, and in other ways, who have never served in any way before and many of these give sacrificially of their time."

Sunday School the Outreach Agency

The church regards the Sunday School as its outreach agency and uses it in every way possible to bring people to the Savior. The Sunday School is staffed with dedicated teachers and leaders and the church leadership seeks to instill in them a sense of responsibility for the souls of people in the community. Training opportunities are provided for teachers and they are encouraged to take advantage of any Sunday School teaching improvement clinic offered on the associational or state convention level. The Sunday School director has served for years and has attended Ridgecrest and Glorieta Conference Centers many times. He is probably as well prepared as the best equipped Sunday School directors to be found anywhere. He is always willing to attempt new things if he feels they will contribute to the growth of the Sunday School and Christ's kingdom.

Graded Worship Services

Another hallmark of this church is the emphasis on the authority of the Word of God. The Bible is accepted as being the divinely, inspired, inherent, infallible word of the almighty God. It is preached from the pulpit and taught in the classroom. It is believed to be the power of God unto salvation to everyone that believeth.

The preaching of the Word is kept central. The house is packed for each service. There is an air of excitement and in a sense expectancy as God's people wait to see what he will do with his Word and bringing conviction to those present. So much so is this true that the church is filled on Sunday evening as well as on Sunday morning.

In order to provide adequately for the worship needs of all the people the Sunday morning schedule provides an extended session for four- and five-year-old children and two graded worship services. One service is for grades one through three; the other for grades four through six. Even in these services the Word is kept central.

Plans for Further Growth

Recently the church utilized the services of the Stewardship Commission of the Southern Baptist Convention in the "Together We Build Program" and in so doing experienced one of the greatest blessings of its 132 years' history. The church had a goal of $130,000 to be applied to the cost of the new building and more than $160,000 was pledged to be paid in three years time. The greatest blessings derived from the program however were not monetary but spiritual. Never before was there such a spirit of oneness and unity among the people as came about as a result of this program. Many members who had shown little or no interest in the church for years became involved in a very definite sense of success and accomplishment characterizes almost all our membership.

The Pastor's Summary

"If any one thing accounts more than any other for the success of this church it would probably be a combination of faith, visions, and hard work." The pastor says, reflecting upon the success of the church. "As a young pastor coming to assume the Amite pastorate I had limited faith and visions. However, through my close association with some of the finest, most dedicated Christian people in the world in the Amite Church, I began to dream dreams and see visions. I came to have goals and visions for the church. As these goals and aims were unfolded and revealed to the people, they adopted them as their own, because the people had a mind to work. A positive attitude and an enthusiastic spirit is instilled in the hearts and minds of God's people; they believe nothing is impossible except that which lies outside the will of God. Bathing all they do in prayer, and seeking the power and presence of the Holy Spirit, they move on from one grand and glorious experience to another.

"Sure, moments of frustrations, futility, and failure have come from time to time. There have been the temptations to quit. I suppose every preacher has experienced such feelings, but God didn't call a single one of his preachers to quit when the going gets rough. At such times I rethink my conversion experience, my call to preach, and my commitment to this church. Then I thank God for a great church and a wonderful people to pastor and for work to do, and I get up and go at it with a renewed determination. Faith, vision, hard work, and the blessings of God are the only ingredients necessary for church growth.

"What does the future hold for Amite Baptist Church? Only God knows the answer to this question. However, we do know that if Amite Church people are as dedicated now and in the future as they have been in the past there can be no doubt they will move forward in a great and mighty way. We now worship and learn in buildings that were parts of dreams for the Amite Church people in the past. Dreams that became reality through sacrifice and dedication. Now it is our turn to thank God for the past and look to the present and future needs of this great church.

"We have just completed construction of a building which has been needed for so long and which proves to be such a blessing to us. In addition, long-range plans call for the construction of a larger sanctuary, hopefully to be begun within the next five years. This is needed if we are to provide adequately for the spiritual needs of the people of our community.

"The continued strong influence of Amite Church is sorely needed in these chaotic and confused times. Therefore, we pledge ourselves to be used for the faithful fulfilling of our mission as a church both here at home and around the world through our mission giving. Whether the Lord returns soon or a thousand years from now may he find Amite Church faithful in carrying on for his glory."

13

Identifying the Characteristics of Churches Reaching People

Does the presence of so many growing Sunday Schools among us promise a new era of Sunday School growth for Southern Baptists? The answer seems to be an affirmative one.

For one thing, the number of growing Sunday Schools gains constantly. Only a few years ago Sunday School enrollment was at a standstill and for several years actually declined. This condition was universal — all the way across the nation, state convention by state convention. A look at the older churches examined in this book shows that several of them experienced this decline. An example is Dauphin Way in Mobile, which suffered a decline of about one hundred in attendance each year for six years. Now Dauphin Way is growing. The encouraging note, however, is that this church is not alone, many others are doing the same. The fifty to sixty churches mentioned in the pages of this book are examples only; the list grows longer month by month.

Typical of the kind of reports that come from churches is one from Pressley Street Baptist Church in Atmore, Alabama. At the time the manuscript for this book was being completed the story of this church came in. After a number of years of decline, it began to grow in the spring and summer of 1973. In the late fall the pastor, Jim Waller, wrote in the church mail-out bulletin, "To God be the glory. Our crowd of 160 souls in Sunday School last Sunday was the second highest in seven years for Pressly Street. The highest was only a few weeks ago when we had 179. God is blessing."

Hopefully, the time will come when every Southern Baptist Sunday School will be a growing Sunday School. In the meantime, the number increases.

In the second place, the necessity of a positive emphasis upon reaching people has been and is being recognized. The characteristic common to the growing Sunday Schools mentioned in this book —

and to all growing Sunday Schools, as far as I can determine — is this commitment. In a sense, this always has been a characteristic attitude of Southern Baptists, both leaders and people. The purpose of the first chapter, the story of Sandy Creek and Shubal Stearnes, is to emphasize this truth. Yet, the classic statements of the Sunday School growth principles contained no explicit statement of the necessity for a positive commitment to reaching people. Neither the "Flake Formula for Sunday School Growth" nor the "Seven Laws of Sunday School Growth" as developed by J. N. Barnette and the then Sunday School staff of the Sunday School Board contained such a statement. Of course, the need for a commitment to reaching people was implicit within the statements themselves, and Sunday School leaders acted on the assumption that the desire and commitment was present.

This was true to a large extent during the years of the fastest Sunday School growth. Perhaps a time came when the laws and principles came to be seen as mechanical means to the end of growth whether or not there existed a depth of commitment to people as people.

The People-to-People basic actions, as developed by Sunday School Board leaders in 1970 and offered to the churches, correctly identified commitment as the beginning point of growth.

This has been borne out by the experiences of the churches. With no exception, pastors say that the growth of their Sunday Schools begin here. Our recognition of this is significant; it helps many other pastors and Sunday School leaders examine their personal commitments and then to lead their churches to do the same.

Of tremendous importance is a thoughtful and deliberate determination by a church that reaching people for Bible study and for Christ is to be its first, foremost, and all-encompassing objective. This priority determines the direction the church program takes. It also affects the attitudes of members toward those who need the ministry of the church.

A third encouraging trend, distinctly noticeable among the churches mentioned in this book, is a conscious use of the traditional Southern Baptist methods of Sunday School growth. The two classic statements of these have been mentioned already.

Among the pastors and ministers of education who lead these

The massive plant of the Dauphin Way Baptist Church of Mobile, Alabama.

Dauphin Way's attendance is climbing through a combination of factors, including a dynamic bus ministry.

churches there is no inclination to question the validity of these methods; nor is there a waste of time in attempting to prove they do not work. Rather, they look upon the methods as proven ways for churches to reach more people and for Bible study — and they use them.

These churches and their leaders have not let the methods become shackles to limit and bind them in building programs and organizations but have used them as wings to free themselves for reaching more people for Bible study. The recognition of certain unchanging principles and methods has in no way stultified or stifled creativity under the Holy Spirit's leadership and guidance. Look at the variety of programs and emphases represented in these churches.

An example is the emphasis upon single adults being made by several of the churches. While some of the details of the program are innovative — advertising in the personal columns of local newspapers — the growth principles are used. Prospects are located, workers are enlisted and trained, the organization is enlarged to make a special place for those who may be reached. Space is provided; it is rearranged and redecorated to appeal to the specific age group which will use it. Contact is established and maintained with each and every person to whom the department ministers. Singles departments often provide special spiritual help in the way of retreats. One of the churches offers its singles a ski retreat, combining the need for fellowship with the need for spiritual refreshment.

Effective bus outreach illustrates the same concept. The bus program that works involves more people in reaching people. It leads to the creation of newer and faster growing teaching units. It calls for better utilization of space. These principles as such were pinpointed for us many years ago. An understanding of the principles makes possible a better bus program reaching more people for Christ.

In a meeting of secretaries and staff members of the state conventions, conducted in late fall, 1973, the statement was made by one of the secretaries: "Pastors and leaders in my state asked me to lead them to understand the proven methods of growth." Others agreed; the same desire was present in all the states.

A fourth promise of growth is akin to the third: a parallel emphasis upon reaching people and providing them with quality Bible teaching. Growing Sunday Schools do not hesitate to emphasize numbers. At the same time they do not fail to emphasize the absolute necessity for quality teaching.

College Heights church has had such a phenomenal growth that it almost sounds unbelievable. Yet, at the same time it emphasizes the need for excellent Bible teaching for every person in attendance. It lovingly insists that every Sunday School teacher be present for the teachers and officers' meeting each week. With a large and well-trained staff of professional leaders, the Dauphin Way church makes a continuing effort to improve the quality of Bible teaching. Yet it never suggests that there is a conflict between quality of teaching and reaching more people; rather it enlarges the organization regularly and prepares for more people year by year.

A further encouraging sign is the increasing emphasis upon evangelism as a Sunday School task and the increasing desire to use the Sunday School as an evangelistic tool. In these growing churches, the lay evangelism school, the continuing witnessing program, and the Sunday School are seen as parts and parcel of the same thrust, the reach out of the church to the lost of the community.

A loss of the spirit of evangelism will bring the growth of a Sunday School to a standstill. Unless that evangelistic thrust becomes real, the Sunday School more and more will minister to its "own kind." A determination that all Sunday School leaders will be offered opportunity to learn to share Christ may well occasion a new beginning.

As great as any other single factor in the growth of these churches is the use of buses for Sunday School outreach. While buses are not necessarily indispensable for growth in all situations, they are the means through which most growing Sunday Schools have expressed their commitment. They also cause commitments to become deeper.

Sunday Schools can grow without using buses. North Phoenix church shows that to be true. Yet, the pastor, Richard Jackson, states without equivocation that he has nothing against buses and rejoices at every story of their success. He says only that bus outreach does not seem the thing for his church at the time he spoke. The First Baptist Church in Columbia, South Carolina, mentioned in chapter 2, has experienced significant growth, but without the use of buses. H. Edwin Young, the pastor, however, has no criticism of those who do.

On the other hand, Landrum Leavell, pastor of First Baptist in Wichita Falls tells his growth story, citing bus program as the major factor in growth. This church, however, now is growing in other areas even faster than in those areas connected with bus outreach.

The bus program offers most churches an opportunity to do faster the things it hopes to accomplish. While it offers victories, the program also presents many problems. Lessons to be learned from these churches which continue to grow through the use of buses include: (1) Make the commitment to reach people; this commitment should precede and support the bus ministry itself. (2) Prepare well before initiating the program; preparation pays rich dividends in avoidance of unnecessary problems and in bringing outstanding success. (3) Enlist and train bus teams for each bus; a team should consist of no less than five people and should include both adults and teenagers. (4) Enlarge the Sunday School organization before the first day the buses run; making provision ahead of time for increased attendance in children and older preschool departments lends stability to the program from the first day. (5) Work every Saturday to reach specific goals the next day; Saturday visitation is the only way to assure success. (6) Plan for children's worship; in most cases children's worship services will be needed and should be planned for from the beginning. (7) Emphasize evangelism; sharing Christ with those who need to know him is the purpose of all the church does.

Often the question is asked, Does the bus outreach program work as well in country churches as in city churches? The answer is that it does. The Amite Baptist Church demonstrates this. The pastor, James K. Pierce, is committed to reaching people, but as he tells of reaching people through the Amite church, he talks of the church's bus program. Appearing in bus clinics in various places, he always speaks of the possibility of an open-country church growing and also of the practicality of its using buses to help achieve that growth.

The use of special high attendance days long was in disfavor with many, yet these fast-growing Sunday Schools use them regularly. Ridgeland Baptist Church achieved the next-to-impossible. It reached from its attendance level of 400 to more than 1,000 on its special day, Super Sunday. Yet, no less amazing was the increase of Guthrie Baptist Church in Guthrie, Kentucky: from 82 to 200 in six weeks.

More than a few churches have doubled their usual attendance on a high attendance day. The First Baptist Church of Paris, Texas, mentioned in chapter 2, is one of these.

Churches using this kind of promotion have discovered that the special day offers several benefits: (1) It generates a spirit of excitement which carries over into other church projects. (2) It involves many people in the promotion and planning, and people-involvement improves the overall program of the church. (3) It furnishes a tool to use in getting every Sunday School member visited. (4) It is a source for discovering many people whose names can be added to the prospect file. (5) It raises the level of Sunday School attendance. (6) It infuses the church with a feeling of victory. Contrary to an often repeated indictment of the high attendance day, the attendance level usually does not drop all the way to the previous level; rather it comes up some with each high attendance effort.

A factor in the growth of these churches, and a fairly constant one, is the personal leadership of the pastor himself. The quality of leadership which seems to mean the most, however, is not so much a dynamic personality as it is a depth of commitment. The people of the churches respond to the depth of the pastor's desire to reach people for Bible study and Christ.

The personal commitment of the pastor, in a sense, is the dynamic of his life. It creates the fire of leadership which makes possible his challenge to the church.

A final factor lifted up for mention here is the sense of excitement which seems to permeate each of these churches. As these express their commitment through bus ministries, through enlarged organizations, and through better Bible teaching, the excitement is born. As the church sets goals and accepts them as challenges, the sense of excitement is heightened. Setting a high attendance goal that requires a miracle to reach creates excitement; reaching the attendance and setting a new record may arouse it to a fever pitch. Seeing people saved and baptized Sunday by Sunday generates more excitement. Bible study is exciting.

When all these things are done with zeal and heartfelt enthusiasm, excitement mounts in a church. It is a holy excitement, arising from the joy of the people in serving the Lord Jesus and in sharing with others through their church and their growing Sunday School.

This is a day of growing Sunday Schools. May the list of the growing ones grow longer each year. To the glory of Christ the Lord. Hallelujah!

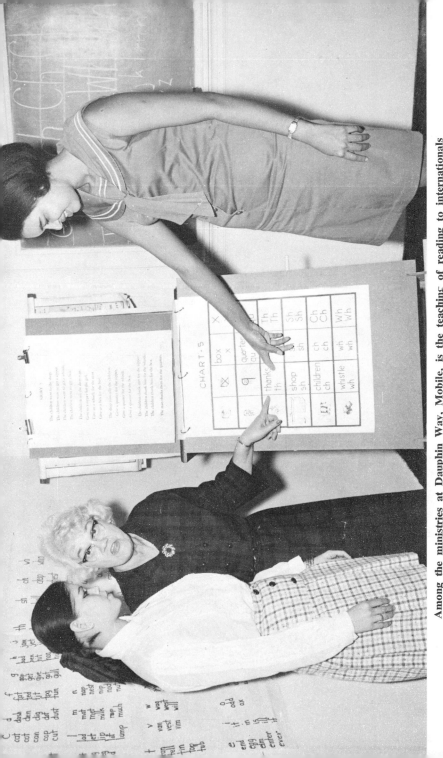

Among the ministries at Dauphin Way, Mobile, is the teaching of reading to internationals via the Laubach method.

Children's church at the Park Avenue Baptist Church, Nashville, Tennessee.

Is everybody ready for mission activities at the Walnut Street Church, Louisville, Kentucky?

Whoops at Walnut Street's skating rink!

Eastwood Baptist Church of Tulsa, Oklahoma, ministers to the total person, including the skinned knee!

Don't be late for the Eastwood bus.

Busses parked at the downtown location of the First Baptist Church, Houston, Texas.

College students flock to classes and special groups at First Church, Houston.

Eugene Skelton, author of this book, and Jim Neyland from Dauphin Way, Mobile, share ideas for Sunday School growth.